ELGAR, NEWMAN AND
THE DREAM OF GERONTIUS

Elgar, Newman and
The Dream of Gerontius

In the Tradition of English Catholicism

PERCY M YOUNG

SCOLAR
PRESS

Published by
SCOLAR PRESS
Gower House
Croft Road
Aldershot
Hants GU11 3HR
England

Ashgate Publishing Company
Old Post Road
Brookfield
Vermont 05036
USA

British Library Cataloguing-in-Publication data
Young, Percy M.
   Elgar, Newman and the "Dream of Gerontius": In the Tradition of
English Catholicism
   I. Title
   782.23092

Library of Congress Cataloging-in-Publication data
Young, Percy M. (Percy Marshall)
   Elgar, Newman and the Dream of Gerontius: in the tradition of
English Catholicism/Percy M. Young.
      p.   cm.
   Includes bibliographical references (p.   ) and index
   ISBN 0–85967–877–6
   1. Elgar, Edward, 1857–1934. Dream of Gerontius.   2. Newman,
John Henry, 1801–1890. Dream of
Gerontius.   3. Oratorios—Analysis. appreciation.   4. Catholic
Church—England—History.   I. Title: Dream of Gerontius.
ML410.E41Y68 1995
782.23—dc20   95–5608
                                 CIP
ISBN 0 85967 877 6

Typeset in Sabon by Photoprint, Torquay, S. Devon
and printed in Great Britain by Biddles Ltd, Guildford

Contents

Illustrations

The cover portraits are reproduced by permission of The National Portrait Gallery and The Elgar Foundation; to the latter, acknowledgement is also due in respect of no 12; for nos 4–7 permission is granted by The Fathers of the Birmingham Oratory; and no. 8 by the Victoria and Albert Museum.

Acknowledgements

I am grateful to the following for their interest and ready assistance:

The Provost and Fathers of the Birmingham Oratory; Mr Gerard Tracey, Archivist, Birmingham Oratory; Rev P T Howell, Diocesan Archivist, Birmingham; Oscott College; the late Father Dennison and St Mary's College; Rev Michael Clifton, Archivist, St George's Cathedral, Southwark; Dominic Minskip, Ushaw College; Ken Simms, Director of Music, Ushaw College; Rev Michael Marsden, St Wilfrid's Church, York; Rev Michael Naylor, The Oratory, London;

Jim Bennett, Elgar Birthplace; Keith Elder, for the loan of the Letters of John Bishop; Jim Davis, Photographic Department, University Library, Birmingham; Professor Alan Douglas; Mrs Mary McInally; Mr N Page; Dr Jan Smaczny; Fr Gregory Winterton; Raymond Monk; Professor Kelsy Thornton;

Duncan Fielden and Stuart Stockley von Statzer, for technical assistance. My wife Renée Morris, without whose daily presence it would not even have been possible to undertake this task.

Percy M Young

Abbreviations

AR	Annual Register
BL	British Library
BWJ	*Berrow's Worcester Journal*
Cath Mag	*Catholic Magazine*
CRS	Catholic Record Society
GM	*Gentleman's Magazine*
Grove	*The New Grove Dictionary of Music and Musicians*
LD	*The Letters and Diaries of John Newman*, ed Charles Dessain et al, London/Oxford, vols I–XXXI, 1961–84
Mawhood	*The Mawhood Diary*
Moore	Jerold Northrop Moore
Mus Brit	Musica Britannica
Mus T	*The Musical Times*
Mus W	*The Musical World*
PRMA	*Proceedings of the Royal Musical Association*
QMM	*Quarterly Music Magazine*
QMMR	*Quarterly Monthly Musical Record*
RCM	Royal College of Music
Rec Hist	*Recusant Histories*

Music ... is the expression of ideas greater and more profound than any in the visible world, ideas, which centre, indeed, in Him whom Catholicism manifests, who is the seat of all beauty, order and perfection whatever.

John Henry Newman, *The Idea of a University*, 1852, Discourse IV, 6

With all reverence we can look for music in the next world – the divine art is divine in this way that it does not seem mean or poor in the most sacred surroundings. We cannot well think of painting or drama in heaven but music we may. Let us fit ourselves by our music in this world to that in the next.

Edward Elgar, *Lecture at Birmingham University*, 29 November 1905

Introduction

For two hundred years the musical appetite of the English people was stimulated by oratorio, and by three works in particular. Handel's *Messiah* reached the nation, so to speak, after the Commemoration of 1784. The provincial choral societies, which developed as a consequence, embraced both this work and Mendelssohn's *Elijah*, after its first performance, in Birmingham in 1846. *The Dream of Gerontius* was described as a masterpiece after its notoriously inadequate first performance – also in Birmingham – in 1900, and fully recognized as such after compelling performances within the two years following.

The oratorios of Handel and Mendelssohn, Old Testament-based, also had their place in the general religious attitudes of the nation. With *The Dream of Gerontius* this was not the case. The text, by John Henry Newman, was not, as in the generality of oratorio texts, concerned with familiar and dramatic episodes from the Old Testament. Being the pattern of a spiritual progress traced in a dream it was inaccessible as narrative. It concerned, however, a concept gaining interest with the publication of Sigmund Freud's *Träumdeutung* in the same year in which *Gerontius* was first performed.

When so many books about Newman have been written, it may seem presumptuous to add to the number. I do so because, in this case, the fact that he was not only musical in a practical sense, but deeply aware of the place of music in life, has received only scant attention. There is, indeed, a case to be made for a critical edition of his writings on the subject. It is not possible to recreate Newman's skill as an instrumentalist, but it is clear that his practical application was lifelong. He also possessed a strong musical creative sense, though of his compositions many did not survive. Of those that have, some examples are given in this book. These betoken Newman's sense of spiritual descent from St Philip Neri, while one small hymn in A minor could have served as a model for the young Elgar.

In *The Catholic Who's Who* of 1913 the entry for Elgar begins:

Elgar, Sir Edward, O M – b 1857 at Broadheath, Worcs, s of W H Elgar, organist. Settled near Worcester as a Prof, and became organist and choirmaster at St George's Catholic church. He subsequently composed and taught music at Malvern.

. . . his *Dream of Gerontius* was produced at the Birmingham Festival of 1900. This masterpiece, hailed immediately as the finest oratorio written by an English pen, after having been performed in Düsseldorf and America, was heard in London for the first time at Westminster Cathedral in 1903, under the baton of the composer.

This notice, updated, remained in *The Catholic Who's Who* to the end of Elgar's life.

Unlike Newman, Elgar was born a Catholic. His education was totally Catholic and his more public musical activities, almost to the time of his marriage, were within a Catholic tradition. As organist of St George's Church he became acquainted with a tradition of church music that had nothing to do with that of the Established Church. His models here were Samuel Webbe and Vincent Novello, Samuel Wesley and William Russell, Mozart and Haydn, Pergolesi and Cherubini, and Beethoven.

The work which is the centre of this study unites the intellectual, theological and cultural properties of English Catholicism, and the first part of the book considers the manner in which English life for three centuries was disturbed, and coloured, by memories of destructive division in the matter of religion. The disadvantages of being Catholic were immense. Discrimination was consistent, with demonstrations against Catholics erupting in Worcester, despite the Act of Toleration of 1829, after William Henry Elgar had arrived in the city.

Elgar himself was not unaware of loud echoes of ancient discrimination before and after the first performance of *Gerontius*. The vicious manner in which both Stanford and Parry derided the work on doctrinal grounds did them no credit. In 1902 the Dean and Chapter of Worcester, in attempting to de-Romanize *Gerontius*, may now be seen to have acted both uncharitably and injudiciously.

The obituary published in *The Musical Times* in April 1934 was by Harvey Grace and William McNaught. They knew Elgar well, and they wrote:

He was not a happy man. His work taxed him body and soul – let the enjoyment he has given to the world be the measure of what it cost him – and its burden was not lightened by his constant and perverse belief that the hand of the world was against him.

So far as biography is concerned, I have considered only those aspects which relate to the history and development of the work. It is not altogether surprising that Newman's poem causes some anguish to the secular mind. Among oratorios it is one of the very few of which any serious account is taken of the argument, or the philosophy, of the libretto. It is, however, the unique union of these words with Elgar's music that constitutes the experience of *The Dream of Gerontius*.

Percy M Young

1 Embassy Chapels

With the death of Handel in 1759 an era in English music came to an end. Almost immediately a fresh impetus was given by the arrival in London – via Germany and Italy – of Johann Christian Bach and Karl Friedrich Abel, and by the cultivation of classical rather than baroque principles. It was no accident that it was during the period in which such principles developed that music assumed fresh significance in the only places of worship in England where Catholic church music could legitimately be performed. These, principally, were the chapels of the Portuguese, Sardinian, Bavarian, Neapolitan and Spanish missions.[1] For fifty years, or thereabouts, these establishments enjoyed two-fold respect: on the one hand for the pastoral facilities afforded to English Catholics; on the other to a broader constituency on account of musical excellence.

In 1760 the music of the Sardinian Chapel received a testimonial from an unexpected direction. In that year John Alcock, Organist of Lichfield Cathedral, under the pseudonym 'John Piper', published a lively, untidy, contentious, humorous novel, *The Adventures of Miss Fanny Brown*. Much of the interest of this work lies in long and critical comments on church and cathedral music, irrelevantly introduced into a generally robust narrative of low life in London. Among the attractions of the city – in which Alcock had once lived – was the music performed at the Chapel of the Sardinian Embassy, the reputation of which persuaded Fanny Brown's three brothers on one Sunday to attend Mass there. After breakfast,

> . . . When they went into the Chapel, a Woman came to them with a Chair each, which *Thomas* and *John* accepted of, but *Henry* drove through the crowd, and kneeled down on the Step at the *Altar* Rails, close to a girl about *Seventeen* years of age, who offer'd him Part of her *Missal* (or Prayer Book) which was *Latin* on one side and *English* on the other. They were all struck with a Reverential awe, as neither of them had ever experienc'd before, at the decent Demeanour of the *Priest*, all the time he was officiating *Mass*, and the serious attention of the whole Congregation . . .

> It being the Feast of St *Bartholomew*, the Organ play'd, and the Singers perform'd an exceeding fine Piece of *Music*, which Thomas was greatly charm'd with, and said he never heard any *Music* go so well before, by the Parts being kept so exactly together.[2]

Taking into account the date of publication of his book, it seems that it was on St Bartholomew's Day (24 August) in 1758 or 1759 that Alcock had attended the service described in such detail. In November 1759 a serious fire destroyed, among other valuables, the early registers of the chapel, its books of plainsong, and some of its sacred vessels and altar linen. During the subsequent period of restoration and renovation, the services of the Chapel were held in the Bull and Gate tavern in Holborn.[3]

At that time there were many German musicians settled in London. Among them was Charles Barbandt, from Hanover, who played the oboe for Handel in his oratorios and also taught music to members of the royal family. In 1755 he dedicated a set of six Sonatas for two violins (or flutes, or oboes) and continuo to the widowed Augusta, Princess of Wales. For her son, George III, Barbandt composed a work that was not only loyal but noisy:

> *God Save Great George The Third Our King: A Loyall Chorus with a Sonata* of three movements] *for the Harpsichord. The Musick most humble* [*sic*] *Dedicated to Their Most Excellent and Illustrious Majesty's* [*sic*].[4]

Whether, like Johann Christian Bach, Barbandt was converted to Catholicism is not known, but in 1764 he became organist of the Chapel of the Bavarian Embassy, where the Ambassador, Baron de Haslang, was a keen lover of music.[5] It was not his appointment as organist, however, that suggests that Barbandt may well have been – or more possibly may have become – a Catholic, but the nature of a small volume of simple, devotional pieces which he published in 1766. These were significant as the first of their kind for Catholic worship to be published in England:

> Sacred Hymns, Anthems and Versicles, for Morning and Evening Service, on all Sundays and Festivals throughout the Year; taken out of the public Liturgy of the Church, and set to Music in a manner no less solemn than easy; and proper to promote the Divine Worship, and excite the Devotion of the faithful.

It was Barbandt's volume of simple pieces – consisting of 29 motets for major Feasts and 55 Latin hymns for Vespers and Compline – composed 'after a French model',[6] for the benefit of singers of modest ability, that began to establish a popular norm for Catholic service music:

Ex. 1

Pange lingua

Through Barbandt, the Bavarian Chapel acquired a temporary celebrity. After this, the music of the Catholic choirs fell to the lowest possible state. It was revived by Mr Webbe; but, 'having generally an imperfect choir to execute his compositions, he seldom struck the higher chords . . .'[7]

Samuel Webbe and William Mawhood

Samuel Webbe was born in Minorca where his father, a Catholic, was a government official. On the death of his father, Webbe came to London, in the first place to be apprenticed to a cabinet-maker. Endowed with musical ability, however, he was brought to the attention of Barbandt. In due course he became Barbandt's apprentice and under his guidance he developed a natural instinct for melodic invention into a general talent for the composition of music for voices.

Through his position at the Embassy Chapel Webbe became friendly with one prominent and cultivated Catholic layman – William Mawhood, a woollen draper – who was influential in respect both of music and political affairs. Since the reign of Charles II a link between sacred and secular music in London had been established by the recognition of St Cecilia's Day on 22 November. In the first instance there was an annual service in St Paul's Cathedral, for which both Purcell and Handel composed major works. In time secular pieces in honour of St Cecilia were composed for the increasingly fashionable Glee and Catch Clubs. The Chapel of the Sardinian Embassy, dedicated to St Cecilia, properly took special pride in the quality of its music. The men of the choir, some being professional musicians, always held a social function on St Cecilia's Day as a charitable fund-raising operation. In this Mawhood, who was well-respected in the City, always played a part. The opening passages of his diary for 1765 indicate a man with an exceptional love of music and considerable skill. On 20 November he attended a meeting of the Madrigal Society, of which he had become a member during the previous year; on the following evening he was present at a concert of the Academy of Ancient Music at the Crown and Anchor tavern; the following Monday, 25 November, he assisted at the St Cecilia's Day celebrations by the Sardinian Chapel singers at the Bull and Gate.

Mawhood's interests in music were far-reaching, extending over the frontier dividing Catholic from Protestant. He went, on the one hand, to the theatre to hear Handel's oratorios,[8] and on the other to the tavern to keep abreast of the new glees and catches. A keen organist, he often deputized at the Sardinian and Bavarian Chapels, and 'opened' new organs: for instance, in the Spanish Embassy Chapel in 1784, in 1790 in the Bavarian Chapel and the new church of St George's in Southwark. On occasion he would play a voluntary after service in St Paul's Cathedral, of which the musicians were among his friends.

In May 1784 Thomas Johnson, a priest of Mawhood's acquaintance, returned from Rome after two years' absence, bringing a new Mass setting of his own. On 27 September John Jones, organist of St Paul's called on Mawhood (presumably by previous arrangement) to collect copies of Johnson's Mass 'to give to Mr Hudson to rehearse over with his boys'. On Sunday 12 December after Vespers at the Sardinian Chapel, Mawhood 'bro[ugh]t home Messrs Dignam and Denby [Danby].[9] We performed the 'Roman' Service'. On the Friday following, 'Mr Hudson of St Paul's, Messrs Moore,[10] Webbe and [Webbe] Junr Mr Danby dined with us; performed the Roman [ie Johnson's] Mass and Arne's Service.'

There would seem to have been, in London at that time, a fine understanding of ecumenical goodwill, considerably influenced by music.

The most notable English composer of the eighteenth century was Thomas Augustine Arne. At the time at which Mawhood's diary begins, Arne was conspicuous in every area of musical life. In summertime his songs were heard nightly in the Pleasure Gardens, and in winter his glees and catches delighted the members of the Glee Clubs. His opera *Artaxerxes* was the only English opera of the period able to compete with those of

Handel. A Catholic, he composed liturgical music for the Sardinian Chapel, where he played the organ.

Two Masses by Arne were in frequent use, an 'Old Service' and a 'New Service'. Of these Masses,

> one [was] in four, the other in three parts; – the latter did not please. The former was exquisite; it was what all church music should be, solemn and impressive; the harmony, correct and simple; the melody slow and graceful. Unfortunately, the thinness of the catholic choirs, in those times, made them drop the contra-tenor and tenor parts, and sing only the canto and base [*sic*]. This entirely spoiled the beauty of the composition.[11]

Of neither of these masses do copies survive. Of a four-part setting of the hymn 'O Salutaris', and a Diurge [*sic*], composed at Mawhood's suggestion in memory of a mutual friend – Francis Pemberton, musician and dancing-master, who died at the beginning of June 1770 – one copy of each remains.[12] On 23 June Mawhood noted that he had 'had a small practice of the Service for Mr Pemberton'. With some additions by Samuel Webbe, the Diurge was performed on 28 June.[13]

The Diurge, *Libera me*, is a landmark in the field of English sacred music, owing nothing to the conventions of the Established Church. Composed for five solo voices with organ accompaniment, it consists of five contrasting sections, Italian in manner, in which the dramatic text is matched by cogent contrasts of texture, rhythm and tonality. Thus the Dies illa section effectively ends:

Ex. 2

Dies illa

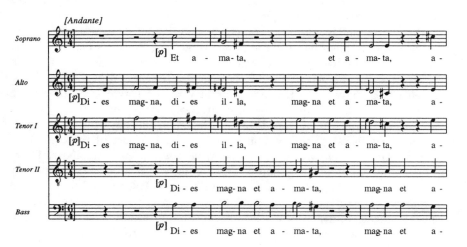

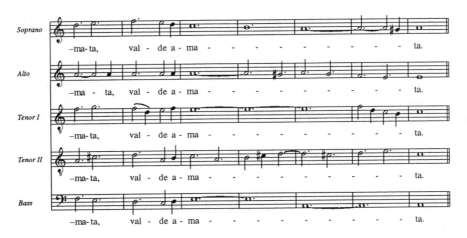

Also associated with the Sardinian Chapel were the Paxton brothers – William and Stephen – the one a virtuoso cellist, the other a popular composer of glees. Stephen[14] shared the composition of one glee, 'Breathe soft, ye winds', with Samuel Webbe. In Webbe's *Collection* of 1792 two Masses and a motet, *Domine salvum fac*, by Stephen Paxton, were published. George Paxton, a nephew of the brothers, followed Arne as organist of the Sardinian Chapel.[15] On 25 October 1775 Stephen Paxton gave to Mawhood the tragic news that George had been drowned 'from a Warf at Black Fryers Bridge'.

On the day following George Paxton's death Webbe called on Dr Peter Browne,[16] the senior chaplain at the Sardinian Embassy, to enquire about the possibility of his filling the vacancy. He reported to Mawhood that he had 'spoken to Dr Brown[e] and got the place if the Embassador does not put in another'. The ambassador was content to take Father Browne's advice, and Webbe's appointment became effective in time for St Cecilia's Day, when the 'special service he has made me [Mawhood] a present of' was sung. Later in the day the 'Gentlemen of the Choir' secularly celebrated St Cecilia at the Queen's Head tavern. In his motet for St Cecilia's Day Webbe displays a characteristic and irresistible charm, particularly apt to the subject.[17]

A group of musically inclined Catholic amateur musicians played no small part in the musical affairs of London in the second part of the eighteenth century. Among them was Charles Butler, who was to be a significant figure in the complex political negotiations, taking place over a period of some fifty years, that led to the passage of the eventual Act of Toleration[18] that relieved Catholics of many of their disabilities. A man truly of the Age of Enlightenment, Butler was a connoisseur of music and a close friend of Mawhood, to whom he lent, and from whom he borrowed, music. On 22

April 1778 he wrote to Mawhood informing him that he proposed the establishment of a Catholic glee party. Whether this did come into being is not known, but on 13 December Mawhood noted: 'Had a Consert of Messrs Paxon [*sic*] & Mrs, Miss [*sic*] Sykes,[19] Webbe, Paxton Junr, Davis, Sacerdos'.

The last-named – Rowland Davies – was said to have been a pupil of Handel, and to have played the organ at the Coronation of George III. Converted to Catholicism he spent some years at Douai before returning to London in 1785 as Chaplain at the Bavarian Embassy.[20] Among other MSS in the Library of Ushaw College, which appear to have been brought back from Rome in the early years of the nineteenth century, is a copy of a fluent *Tantum ergo* for two sopranos and organ, in two short movements, dated 1780, by the Reverend Rowland Davies.

Ex. 3a

Tantum ergo

Ex. 3b

Genitori Genitoque

In his day Samuel Webbe was at the centre of virtually all part-singing activity in London, as composer of sorely needed church music and of excellent (and cheerful) glees. His celebrated geniality, however, covered areas of personal difficulty; at such times it is clear that he was much helped by Mawhood. There is one episode in Webbe's life referred to by Mawhood about which silence was generally maintained. Taken mysteriously ill in September 1779, he was even 'said to be dying'. As it was, however, he made a full recovery, to live another thirty-seven years. Looking forward to a new lease of life, he promptly composed a mass to commemorate the consecration of a new choir gallery in the Sardinian Chapel. One may suspect the cause of Webbe's breakdown to have been of a psychological rather than a physical nature, for domestic circumstances were clearly distressful. His marriage had, for whatever reason, come to an end.[21]

At this point Webbe's concerns were swept aside by political developments. In 1778 an address on behalf of a representative body of Roman Catholic Peers and 163 Commoners had been presented to Parliament by the Earl of Surrey, and Lords Linton and Petre. The address stated:

> Our exclusion from many of the benefits of [the] Constitution has not diminished our reverence for it. We have thoughtfully received such relaxation of the rigour of the laws, as the mildness of an *enlightened* age, and the benignity of your Majesty's government, have gradually produced. But we cannot wait for ever.[22]

The passage through Parliament of a Catholic Relief Act, commended by Edmund Burke in the interests both of England and Ireland, and introduced by Sir George Savile on 14 May 1770, 'for relieving his Majesty's Subjects professing the Popish Religion from certain Penalties and Disabilities imposed on them by an Act made in the Eleventh and Twelfth Years of the Reign of King William the Third . . .' alerted Protestant objectors. When, in 1778, it was proposed to extend the Act to include Scotland the prospect 'spread an immediate alarm throughout that country'.[23] The matter was under debate in Parliament when, on 2 June 1780, incited and led by Lord George Gordon, 'subscribers to the petition of the Protestant Association, praying a repeal of the late Act in favour of the Roman Catholics', took to the streets in their thousands. The riots that followed were the worst in English history.

On Friday, 2 June

> The mob paraded off in different divisions from Palace-yard, and some of them went to the Romish Chapel in Duke-street, Lincolns-inn-fields, others to that in Warwick-street, Golden-square, both of which they in a great measure demolished . . .

There was some diminution of violence on Saturday; but worse was to follow.

> On Sunday in the afternoon, the rioters assembled again in large bodies, and attacked the dwelling-houses of the catholics in and about Moorfields. They stripped their chapels not only of the ornaments and insignia of religion, but tore up the altars. pulpits, pews, and benches, and made fires of them, leaving nothing but the bare wall.[24]

And so it continued, with the homes of prominent supporters of the Act being destroyed. One day it was the house of Sir George Savile, on another the home of Lord and Lady Mansfield, where the books in the library and the pictures on the walls were burned, while the wine in the cellars was distributed among the mob. Prisoners were released and prisons set on fire. Where there were Catholic businesses they were especially sought out. One night The Ship alehouse, in Lincoln's Inn Fields, was demolished, 'on account of their suffering mass to be said there on Sunday last'. On another the distillery and some houses belonging to Mr Langdale, a prominent Catholic, were set alight – with thirty-six fires, all blazing. At one time Bishop Challoner, the aged vicar apostolic, was in great danger, until taken to timely safety at Mawhood's house in the country. Finally, when martial law had been imposed, the riots died away and Lord George Gordon, the author of the troubles, was eventually seized and committed as a prisoner to the Tower. On trial he was acquitted. Finally, having subsequently been committed to Newgate for libelling the judiciary, he died insane in 1787.

The consequences of the Gordon Riots – in destruction of public buildings, and of private houses, in loss of life, and in the severity of the sentences passed by the judges – were horrendous. But the twenty years remaining of the eighteenth century were to bring a cautious extension of toleration. A mark of improvement in Catholic morale came with a signal act of respect shown for the authority of the Crown in 1788, when it was announced that, as well as in churches, synagogues, and the Dutch Church, 'Prayers [are] to be said for the Recovery of the King's Health, in the Chapels of the Roman Catholics . . . for our most beloved King George.' At the same time the last dynastic impediment to the monarchy was removed by the recent death of Charles Edward Stuart, Duke of Albany.[25]

For Samuel Webbe, the last two decades of the eighteenth century offered him greater opportunity and gained for him increasing respect. By 1782 the outlook for Catholics was already more hopeful and, when worship no longer needed to be clandestine, the publication of appropriate music was timely. In that year, in an anonymously published *Essay on the Church Plain Chant*, Webbe attempted to out-Merbecke Merbecke in presenting, in plainsong notation, melodies later to become generally popular.

Ex. 4

O Salutaris

Easily accommodated in *Hymns Ancient and Modern* (1861) to a hymn from John Keble's *Christian Year*, 'O Salutaris' was followed into the wider fields by 'Veni sancte spiritus' ('Come, Thou Holy Spirit, come'), and 'Another Prose on the Nativity of our Lord' ('O come all ye faithful'). Webbe was well supported by his friends and colleagues. Among the subscribers to the *Collection of Masses* (1792) were at least six of the priests of the Sardinian Chapel, headed by Father Browne, and many of the parishioners named in Mawhood's Diary.

His music easily crossed doctrinal frontiers and there is a touching serenity about the contents of *Twelve Anthems particularly calculated for Families or small Choral Societies*, published by Birchall (1798?). These, in the manner of motet rather than of anthem in the Anglican style, were introduced in this manner:

> The following little Pieces are humbly submitted to the Perusal of those who on Days set apart for Devotion, might wish to take the Aid of Music, in raising the Mind to a Contemplation of the DIVINE GOODNESS in Man . . . In Order to render them the more useful for Families, or private musical Parties, they seldom require more than Three Voices; but the Effect may be considerably improved by more Voices joining in those Places marked TUTTI . . .

In some of these pieces and, in particular, in 'Evening Devotion' is a sense of the necessary, familial privacy of Catholic worship of not far distant times, and of the devotional inspiration of Bishop Challoner's 'The Garden of the Soul'. There is also even a hint of Purcell's Evening Hymn.

Ex. 5

Evening Devotion: 'The Day is Thine . . .'

Popular throughout the profession and among all glee singers, Webbe became Librarian of the Glee Club (1787), Secretary of the Nobleman's Catch and Glee Club (1794), and one of the founders of the Concentores Sodales (1797), for which society he composed another cheerful tribute to St Cecilia in an intimate setting of Dryden's 'Divine Cecilia' – a companion piece to his Cecilian Motet.

The artlessness of Webbe's glee style transferred itself naturally into his church music. Thus he became the initiator of a style of Catholic church music which, being considered practicable for small (often irregular) groups of inexpert singers – women rather than boys for the treble and alto parts – was fundamentally different from that of the Church of England. He understood too a didactic influence to lie in music, which – while it should not be too demanding of the limited skills of Catholic choristers – should not lack diversity of colour. Within the limits of his canvas Webbe was often subtly able to convey a timely Romantic atmosphere, within which he could effectively convey to the untutored the meaning of the Faith:

Ex. 6

Ascendit Deus in Jubilo

In 1819 James Taylor, of Norwich, neatly approved Webbe's aims and achievement:

> He was well aware that music, in many parts, enriched with extraneous modulations, is not to be performed but by singers whose powers and abilities are of the very first rate; that such music is much better calculated for the chamber than the church, and that such choirs could not be expected out of London. He therefore so calculated his music as to produce, even in small choirs, a choral effect.[26]

Equally felicitous is William Barrett's appreciation:

> The varied manner in which he set the words of the text of the Mass for the service of the Roman Catholic Church would alone give sufficient evidence of the care and consideration with which he approached his musical labours. This evident anxiety to lose no point of the meaning of the words may account for the total difference of setting of words in all his Masses, his chief contribution to sacred music.[27]

Vincent Novello

Webbe was acknowledged to be a good teacher. His most conspicuous pupil was Vincent Novello, son of an immigrant Piedmontese pastry-cook and an English mother. He was baptized in the Chapel of the Neapolitan Embassy and, after a brief schooling in France, enrolled as a chorister in the Sardinian Chapel. Tutored by Webbe, for whom he deputized when necessary, and encouraged by Danby at the Spanish Chapel, he progressed to the point at which, at the age of sixteen, he was considered competent to undertake the post of Organist at the Portuguese Embassy Chapel.

Here Novello remained for twenty-five years, during which he not only powerfully influenced English music in general but also ensured that the English Catholic Church would be able to fashion an independent order for its music, based on tradition, on European relationships, and on practicality. Drawn by the music performed at the Portuguese Chapel under his inspiration, and not to be heard elsewhere, many non-Catholic music-lovers as well as professional musicians regularly came to augment both the normal congregations of the chapel and, at the same time, its funds.

Novello's daughter Mary recalls these services:

> On Sundays I knelt beside my mother in the Portuguese Embassy's Chapel, South Street, Grosvenor Square . . . . A central figure in the picture that small sanctuary has painted on my memory is that of my godfather, the Reverend William Victor Fryer, as he officiated at the altar, irradiated by the light from the tall wax candles thereon, and when he stood in the pulpit delivering the sermon . . . .
> [Novello's] organ-playing attained such renown that it attracted numerous persons, even among the nobility, whose carriages waited for them outside, while they lingered at the end of the service, and after; for it was playfully said that his 'voluntaries' – intended to 'play out' the congregation – on the contrary, kept them in, listening to the very last note.[28]

As he became increasingly influential from his post at the Portuguese Chapel, Novello also became concerned for the generally deplorable state of Catholic church music. He also became aware of the activities of Christian Ignatius Latrobe (1757–1836), son of the founder of a community of exiled Moravian Brethren settled at Fulneck, in Yorkshire, and Secretary to the Unity of the Brethren in England. There were few in England so well informed in matters relating to European sacred music than Latrobe. He was friendly with Haydn, to whom he dedicated three sonatas, and whose influence is present in a dramatic setting of the *Dies Irae*. Between 1806 and 1818 Latrobe published a three-volume *Selection of Sacred Music, from the Works of the Most Eminent Composers of Germany and Italy*, dedicated to the Princess Charlotte. Among the composers represented were C P E Bach, Caldara, C H Graun, J A Hasse, Michael and Joseph Haydn, Mozart and Pergolesi.

Novello, who had assembled and edited material for use in the Portuguese Chapel, decided himself to undertake publication of suitable music for general Catholic use. In 1811, in mind of Webbe's *Collection of*

Sacred Music as used in the Chapel of the King of Sardinia in London, he commenced his career as publisher with *A Collection of/Sacred Music/as performed in the/Royal Portuguese Chapel/in London.*

The origin of the Collection, starting from his 'own little compositions' and expanded through 'the masterly productions of Mozart, Haydn, Durante etc,' suitably edited, was explained in a preliminary advertisement:

> Most of the following Pieces were written at different intervals for the sole use of the Portuguese Chapel and without any view to future Publication; but from having been found not ill-adapted to the Powers of a small Choir, and more particularly in consequence of the very great scarcity of similar productions, so many applications were made from Persons who were desirous of possessing Copies, that at last I resolved to alter my original intention and to publish them.

At the time there was a growing tendency to abolish the alto and tenor C clefs in favour of the treble clef. Novello's reason for not so doing derives from philosophy rather than from methodology:

> . . . The Treble Clef when applied to the Counter & Tenor parts, does not indicate the real or true notes that are required to be sung. The C Clef does, and I trust therefore that no Apology is necessary on my part for preferring Truth to Falsehood, or that which is proper, to that which is improper.

Dedicated to Rev W V Fryer, this crusading work attracted much goodwill from subscribers. Among them, perhaps surprisingly, were the Royal Dukes of Kent, Cambridge, and Gloucester, and the Princesses Mary and Sophia. Of prominent Catholics there were Bishops John Milner, Vicar Apostolic of the Midland District, and William Poynter of London, John Nyren, the cricketer – close friend of the Novello family and one of the first to foretell the future fame of Clara – and Robert Berkeley,[29] from Worcestershire.

The large number of musicians subscribing testified to the respect in which Novello was held in the profession. Among them were Thomas Attwood of St Paul's, Charles Burney, Benjamin Jacob – co-worker with Samuel Wesley in the cause of 'John Sebastian Bach' – the composers William Russell and William Shield, and Samuel Picart – a Bach-loving Prebendary of Hereford, acquainted with Novello through their mutual friend Samuel Wesley.

Published at an opportune time, Novello's *Collection* (reissued in 1825) encouraged compilation of various anthologies for Catholic use, as well as others of more general interest, which appeared during Novello's term of office at the Portuguese Chapel. Volumes containing works by Purcell, and by Carissimi, Clari, Durante, Jomelli, Leo, Palestrina, Pergolesi and other Italian composers in *Fitzwilliam Music* were to open doors to wide expanses of music hitherto unexplored in England.

Having undertaken the duty of providing English Catholics with a new musical literature – on the one hand representing the best that could be made available, and on the other that which suited the means at the disposal of the parish chapel (rather than the Embassy Chapel) – Novello went methodically forward. Three volumes of *Twelve Easy Masses, calculated for Small Choirs* – dedicated to Lord Arundell[30] – were published in 1816. In 1819 there were six volumes of *Motets for the Offertory*, and *for the Morning Service*. Four years later *Hymns for the Evening Service* appeared, in which – as well as pieces by many of the European composers made familiar by Latrobe – works by Samuel Wesley, William Russell and Novello himself were included. The direction which Novello took – away from English expectations of 'sacred music' – helped to infuse into the tradition variety of colour and of expression. William Russell's *Miserere mei*, contributed to Novello's *Motets for the Offertory*, is a singularly affecting miniature well suited to the classical company with which it was offered:

Ex. 7

Miserere mei

In the Preface to his *Selection of Sacred Music* Latrobe replied to a 'German author', who had complained of an apparent lack of interest in Mozart in England, by saying that, while Mozart 'was not universally known in his true greatness', it had to be said that 'in this country we cannot do justice to his Compositions for the Church, which therefore remain unknown to the English Public'. This opinion influenced Novello to include isolated movements from Mozart in his collections of 1811 and 1816. By 1817 he was vigorously occupied in the preparation of a volume of Masses by Mozart. Concerned that he should only publish what was authentic, he sought Latrobe's assistance and obtained from him the copies that he used as the basis of a collection. Finally, in 1819, assured by a long and detailed letter from Latrobe, Novello was able to issue the main part of what, over the years, was to become a complete edition.

These Masses became exceedingly popular (not only for liturgical use, but also among choral societies). The most popular was the 'Twelfth', which was copied 'from a MS in the possession of Edmund Harris, Organist of a Catholic Chapel at Bath'.[31] That this work, being singable, was found not to be authentic did not disturb its place in the popular repertory.

On 12 September 1821 Novello received the following letter from Samuel Webbe junior, now organist at the Spanish Embassy Chapel:

> I have had the satisfaction to understand that your worthy labours in the adaptation of Mozart's Masses have been substantially acknowledged by the musical public. I trouble you with this note to inquire whether you have a similar design in contemplation with regard to those of Haydn.
>
> Should it appear that you have not – I shall probably bestow some attention upon them myself – as they appear to me fully entitled to their share of publicity.
>
> > Yours truly
> > Sam Webbe
> > 48 Woburn Place[32]

On 11 December of the same year Dr William Crotch 'presented his compliments to Mr V Novello and begs to thank him for his kind present of the first number of Haydn's Masses'.[33] Between 1823 and 1825 Novello completed his edition of those works.

The last Mozart Masses, nos 16, 17, 18, were published in March 1824. A few weeks later Novello resigned his post at the Portuguese Chapel. Two years later the function of the chapel was ended by the death of the King of Portugal. On 22 April a 'solemn funeral service' was performed at the Chapel, the music, chosen by His Excellency the Marquess Palmella [Ambassador] being selected from Masses of Mozart, Cherubini, and Jomelli. The principal singers were Mlle Marinoni, Mrs Hunt, Begrez, Pearman, 'and a singer with an exquisite tenor voice of the name of Giubilei'. The orchestra included the generally indispensible cellists, Spagnoletti and Lindley, and the double bass virtuoso, Dragonetti.[34]

In a brilliant series of essays in *The Musical Times*, Edward Holmes provided an Introduction to Novello's edition of Mozart's Masses, characteristically reflecting also on the manner in which Novello (and his brother) had brought together the interests of those who patronized the

Italian Opera, those who belonged to the newly founded Philharmonic Society, those who patronized the Antient Concerts and the Oratorios, and those whose first interest was in sacred music:

> The connecting link between Mozart the dramatic composer, and Mozart in his masses, was Mr Frank Novello, formerly prompter at the opera in the palmy days of Taylor's management, and also principal bass at the Portuguese Ambassador's Chapel in South-Street, Grosvenor-Square, where his brother was organist. This gentleman, whose talents and amiable enjoying disposition still preserve his memory in the lively affection and esteem of his acquaintance, was an admirable chamber singer, and particularly excelled in Mozart's music, which he sang with the same accent and inflections of tone as Dragonetti on his bass. The enthusiasm created by Mozart at the Opera on Saturday was thus easily transferred to the Mass performed at South-Street on Sunday. And most admirable performances there were of Nos 1, 2, 7, with portions of others now difficult to indicate.
>
> The Quartet singing of Mrs Hunt, Evans (alto), Gattie (tenor), and F Novello (bass), was animated by so perfect a delight in the new style of music, and restrained by such judgement and knowledge of effect, that it seemed impossible to attain higher unity or exactitude of expression from four voices. . . .The choir at South-Street, though small, had grandeur of effect in the execution of fine compositions, because it was well proportioned to the locality. The organ, an old instrument in its diapasons, with very fine modern additions in the swell and reed work, was certainly of a size disproportioned to the chapel. Yet though one wished it better placed, under the hands of Mr Novello it produced noble and varied effects; and the chorus was accompanied by him with a precision and *aplomb*, in which he was never excelled. A very great enthusiasm possessed this excellent artist, who was never known to tire of music. . .[35]

A less formal recognition of Novello's worth is contained in an undated letter from Charles Lamb to his former school friend George Dyer:

Cliffords Inn

Dear Dyer:

My very good friend, and Charles Clarke's father in law, Vincent Novello, wishes to shake hands with you. Make him play you a tune. He is a damn'd fine musician, and what is better, a good man and true. He will tell you how glad we should be to have Miss Dyer & you here [Enfield] for a few days. Our young friend Miss [Emma] Isola has been here holy day making, but leaves us tomorrow.

Yours ever, Ch. Lamb.[36]

Notes

1 The Portuguese Embassy Chapel, the oldest of such institutions, was established in consequence of the marriage of Charles II to Catharine of

Braganza in 1662. First situated in Lincoln's Inn Fields, it moved successively to Golden Square (Warwick Street), and to South Street. In 1719 the Sardinian Embassy took the Lincoln's Inn Fields tenancy, while in 1736 the Bavarian Chapel moved into the premises in Golden Square. A new building for the Bavarian Chapel (which, like the Sardinian, was destroyed during the Gordon Riots) was opened in 1788. This in due course became the Church of Our Lady of the Assumption and St Gregory. St James's Church, Spanish Place, now occupies the site of the former Spanish Embassy Chapel.

2   *The Adventures of Miss Fanny Brown*, XXVI, pp 186, 192: Alcock compared the music of the Established Church unfavourably:

> I wish I could say our Cathedrals and Churches were as well regulated, and taken Care of; it being notorious to any strict Observer, that there are hardly two of our *Choirs* that chant the *Liturgy* alike; And, tho' formerly the *Music* of the *Church*, *Chamber*, and *Theatre* were always perform'd very different from each other; yet now, they may with great truth be said, to be all united; As the *Theatric* Taste prevails even in the *Church* and *Chamber*.

3   Farrell, J K A, *The Church of St Anselm and St Cecilia*, Burlington Press, Bristol, 1967, p 6.

4   BL, RM 21.e.33.

5   Haslang died on 29 May 1783, aet.83, and was buried at St Pancras cemetery.

6   Stafford, W C, *History of Music*, Constable, Edinburgh, 1830, p 376.

7   Butler, Charles, *Historical Memories of the English, Irish, and Scottish Catholics, Since the Reformation*, 4 vols, London 1822, IV, Xcviii. 5 'The Sacred Music of the English Catholic Church', p 463.

8   *The Orthodox Journal and Catholic Monthly Intelligencer*, IV, 1816, for doubts on the propriety of Catholics attending performances of Handel's oratorios, see letters on pp 436, 483, 486.

9   Robert Hudson, vicar-choral at St Paul's in 1756, almoner and master of the children 1773–1793; Charles Dignum, one of Webbe's choristers, a popular tenor and member of the Bavarian Chapel choir; John Danby, a chorister in the Sardinian Chapel, became organist of the Spanish Chapel, where, after his death in 1798, Webbe took over some of the duties. Danby's fourth book of Glees was published posthumously 'for the Benefit of his Widow and Four Infant Children'. His daughter Caroline married H G Nixon (1796–1849), see Chapter 3, n 8.

10 Rev John Moore, Rector of St Bartholomew-the-Great, in which parish Mawhood lived.

11 [Arne] composed two masses ['Services'] for the Sardinian Embassy choir – 'one in four, the other in three parts – the latter did not please. The former was exquisite; it was what all church music should be, solemn and impressive; the harmony, correct and simple; the melody slow and graceful. Unfortunately, the thinness of the catholic choirs, in those times, made them drop the contratenor and tenor parts, and sing only the canto and base [*sic*]. This entirely spoiled the beauty of the composition.' Butler, op.cit., p 462.

12 *O Salutaris*, BL, Add MS 31806; *Libera me*, Add MS 33240. It was believed that a chorister of the Sardinian Chapel collected MSS by Arne and took them to Rome to present to Henry Benedict Stuart, Cardinal of York, brother of

Charles Edward. Hubert Langley, *Doctor Arne*, Cambridge 1938, p 97, cf fn 25.

13 Francis Pemberton married Mary Castell on 4 June 1739, Arne's wife, Anne being a witness (*CRS*, XIX, p 175). Mawhood's sons were taught dancing by Pemberton. The score of *Libera me*, which passed to Vincent Novello was presented by him to the Musical Antiquarian Society in 1849. On the score are the names of these singers: Swiney (S), Fitz (A), Lanza (CT), Guich^d (T), and [Francis] Novello (B).

14 'a zealous and good Roman Catholic', R J S Stevens, *Recollections* Macmillan, (ed Mark Argent), London 1992, p 28.

15 He was organist on Christmas Day 1767, when one of Arne's Masses was performed. Mawhood, p 27.

16 Father Peter Browne (1730–1794), of Irish-English parentage, born in Oporto, Portugal, and educated at Douai, was chaplain at the Sardinian Embassy in 1760, agent for the clergy of the ecclesiastical Middle District of England in 1770, and dean of the chapter in 1789. He was in charge of the chapel at the time of the Gordon Riots.

17 St Cecilia's Day motet, *A Collection of Sacred Music as used in the Chapel of the King of Sardinia in London*, 1785, p 15.

18 'He was a very good judge of Music, and could *justly* appreciate such rare and tasteful productions as those by Carissimi, Clari, Stradella, Durante, Steffani & other great masters of the *sterling* Italian school of composition.' Samuel Wesley, of Charles Butler, to Vincent Novello: BL, Add MS 11729, f 36.

19 Perhaps related to Sykes, organist of the Portuguese Embassy Chapel.

20 Mawhood, p 135, fn 3.

21 Thomas Horrabin, agent for the College at St Omer, promised Mawhood that he would write to Father Wilkinson, president of the College at St Omer, asking if Mrs Webbe could be given 'accomodation'. Mrs Webbe, who 'owns her fault' (Diary 23 April), but supported by a pension from Webbe, retired to France. The two daughters were placed in the English nunnery in Bruges, but 'not giving content' to their teachers were removed, to be looked after by their mother. Mawhood, p 199, July 1783.

22 AR, 1778, State Papers, p 301.

23 ibid, 1780, p 190.

24 ibid, p 259f.

25 Charles Edward Stuart was the elder son of James Francis Edward Stuart (1688–1766), Chevalier St George, son of James II by his second wife, Mary of Modena. He married Maria Clementine Sobieski in 1719. The funeral, at which 'some of the best voices from Rome' sang, took place in the cathedral of Frascati, of which diocese the brother of the deceased, Henry Benedict, Cardinal Duke of York, was Bishop (*AR* p 253–255). Between 1786 and 1788 Thomas Greatorex visited Charles Edward in Rome and obtained from him a number of musical MSS, including seven volumes of 90 Italian cantatas by A Scarlatti; see A Hyatt King, *Some British Collectors of Music*, London, 1963, p 37.

26 James Taylor, letter in *QMM*, 1819, p 297–301, 'hazards an opinion as to how it happens that his sacred music is generally considered inferior to his secular compositions' . . . for Taylor, however, it is clear that 'Mr Webbe has not descended in his sacred music'.

27 Barrett, William Alex, *English Glees and Part-Songs*, London 1886, p 224.

28 Cowden-Clarke, Mary, *My long Life*, London 1896 , p 10. William Victor Fryer DD, (b Somerset 1765, ob 9 Sept 1844). Educated at English College, Lisbon, where his uncle had been President; principal chaplain at Portuguese Chapel; retained chaplaincy after closure of chapel. In 1828 Fryer and his protégé William Placid Morris were presented to Don Miguel, Regent of Portugal, shortly before the closure of the chapel.

29 Robert Berkeley (1764–1845), of Spetchley Park, near Worcester, was father of Robert Berkeley (1794–1879). See Chapter 7, n 10.

30 James Everard, Baron of Wardour, patron of John Francis Prina, 'a pupil of Mr Novello, and was entrusted with the important duty of organist at the Portuguese Chapel at the early age of ten years. His talent and amiable manners acquired for him the kindly patronage of Lord Arundell, in whose mansion he resided for a considerable length of time', *Mus W*, New series CXCIII, no CCLXXXV, Sept 9, 1841.

31 Former Theatre Royal, converted to Chapel in 1809, subsequently Freemasons' Hall.

32 Samuel Webbe Junr (c 1770–1843): 1798, Organist of Liverpool Unitarian Chapel, 1817, Spanish Embassy Chapel; subsequently St Nicholas and St Patrick's RC chapel, Liverpool; editor *Convito Armonico*, 2 vols glees (1808–23).

33 BL, Add MS 11730, p 292.

34 *Harmonicon*, 1826, p 94.

35 *Musical Times*, Vol 5, October 1852–March 1853.

36 BL, Add MS 11730, f 104.

2 The Influence of Novello and Wesley

In 1819 William Placid Morris OSB,[1] one of Bishop John Milner's protégés, was assigned to duty in the London District, where he was to work for ten years as an assistant to Victor Fryer. Being musical, it was a particular pleasure to be associated with the Portuguese Chapel. But as the political situation in Portugal deteriorated, the future of the Embassy itself became increasingly uncertain. In 1828 Fryer and Morris met with the then ruler of Portugal, Dom Miguel – who, having undertaken to act as Regent on behalf of his under-age niece, Maria da Glória, seized the throne for himself. In a period of instability, during which the usurper was, with British aid, removed, the Embassy in London ceased to function. The chapel itself – the lease from the Duke of Westminster having expired – was already closed.

In the summer of 1829 Vincent Novello and his wife travelled to Salzburg in order to present to Mozart's aged and indigent sister, Frau Maria Anna Sonnenberg, a gift of money subscribed by English admirers of her brother. In the spring of the next year she died. As the Chapel of the Portuguese Embassy was not yet out of commission, Novello was able to arrange in her memory a performance of her brother's Requiem, with a professional group of singers and instrumentalists. In its last days – with Vincent Novello once more assuming his former office – this was an occasion which worthily recalled the former importance of the chapel as a musical centre:

> Eye as well as ear was gratified upon that occasion (the last wherein the South Street Chapel shone with its former glory; for, soon after, it was dismantled, and the Embassy's service no longer performed there) in the expression of Vincent Novello's countenance, while the reflection of the light from the tapers fell upon it, beaming with intellectual rapture and enthusiasm for the great master he was illustrating, as well as for the art in which he himself so excelled.[2]

Novello's influence, particularly through his direction of the music at the Portuguese Embassy Chapel, can hardly be underestimated. For better or worse, the style of music popularized there settled the aims of Roman Catholic musicians in Britain for the greater part of the nineteenth century. From the beginning there was a dramatic quality in the music heard, which was enhanced by the setting and the ceremonial. The singers employed (many of them being attuned to Italian opera, either as within their birthright or, if British, through rare opportunity) recognized a duty in releasing the theatrical nature of the most popular music in the Catholic repertory.

Although Novello was recognized as the pioneer in respect of sacred music, excellent performances were increasingly heard in other places. The better they were, the more there was complaint from the unmusical and the pietistic. On 2 March 1816 one 'Palatinus' wrote to the *Gentleman's Magazine*, objecting to a concert which mixed Nathan's recently published settings of Byron's *Hebrew Melodies* with popular songs of the day and ending with the 'Gloria Patri':

> If this spirit confined itself to the concert-room it would have been well; but it is notorious, and a subject of deep regret to all real friends of the Establishment, that the present music in the fashionable Chapels in the West end of the town is a shocking mixture of sacred and profane. Will the congregation in country churches believe that the music to some of the Psalms is played to resemble the thunder of the Almighty – often the roaring of the waves? Yet that is really the fact.[3]

Two years later a note, possibly from Charles Butler, testified to the quality of the performances at the Bavarian Embassy:

> Even in this era of musical excellence, it may be doubted whether those who have not heard the service performed as it now is by Begrez, by Garcia, and Naldi, have not heard the most perfect singing which England possesses.[4]

But it is clear that good taste did not always prevail. Manuel Garcia – the most famous tenor of the day in England – did not confine his talents to performance. He also composed comic operas and, in similar style, masses. As long as he was to be heard, 'the town flocked to Warwick-street Chapel to hear a mass composed by Signor Garcia, the tenor singer at the opera'.[5]

Sometimes, however, it could be pointed out that even in Germany performances of sacred music could be affected by lapses in judgment. Edward Holmes recalled hearing a Mass of Haydn in B flat in the cathedral in Munich, a performance which he did not compare favourably with what he had heard in one of the London chapels:

> Many movements were played in a time utterly distinct from that which is generally received in London as the correct one. The Benedictus ... was taken much too fast; but it is more likely that the priests might be blameable

for hurrying the music, than that the director misunderstood its character
.... The soft stops of the organ blended charmingly with the stringed
instruments; but the organist was rather deficient in taste, and his playing
made me lament the manner in which I have heard the same thing executed
on a pianoforte in England.[6]

Italian opera singers moved in and out of London and, during the first
half of the nineteenth century, were not infrequently persuaded to sing at
services in the Sardinian chapel. At the funeral of the sister of Giulia Grisi,
Lablache, Rubini, Tamburini, Persiani and Grisi herself sang.[7] By courtesy
of the Embassy, the chapel by now had come to serve as a parish church
for Catholics resident in the area of Lincoln's Inn Fields.

In the somewhat freer climate that obtained after the passing of the Act
of Catholic Toleration in 1829, opportunities for singers (not necessarily
Catholic by conviction) multiplied, so that on Easter Sunday it could be
said that mass was usually accompanied 'by compositions of the most
brilliant character'. On that day in 1836 the soloists at the Bavarian and
Spanish Chapels respectively were Thomas Cooke and Henry Phillips, and
Clara Novello and Richard Bellamy; at the Sardinian Chapel there was to
be heard a 'new Mass by Mr Guynemer'; at St Patrick's Church in Soho,
Haydn's third Mass 'with full band'; and at St George's-in-the-Fields,
another of Haydn's Masses.[8]

Among those who had played a conspicuous part in helping to promote
the legislation that, after many years of fevered debate, had culminated in
the passage of the Act of 1829, was Lord Henry Peter Brougham, at
various times Lord Chancellor. In this manner, as subsequently reported in
Dublin, he set out to testify to his personal belief in the meaning of
toleration:

> The Chancellor of England, Lord Brougham, attended the Catholic chapel
> in Warwick-street, London, on Saturday 13th July [1834]. His Lordship was
> in the Hon. E. Petre's pew, with Lady Petre and Lord Stafford, her Ladyship's
> father. High Mass was celebrated, and Mozart's Mass, No. 12, was sung
> with a full choir. The solo parts were taken by Madam Garcia [*sic*] , Mrs.
> Bishop, Signor Begrez, Mr. Bedford, and Mr. T. Cooke.
> The Protestants have nearly got mad at the Lord Chancellor thus
> attending High Mass.[9]

On Whitsunday 1838 the celebrated Leicester amateur musician, and
commentator on musical events, William Gardiner, with friends, made a
musical tour of London. After Morning Service at Westminster Abbey,
they drove to

> the Bavarian Chapel, and, by the aid of eighteen pence each, obtained an
> uncomfortable seat. Here the masses of Haydn and Mozart are as well
> executed as the mere accompaniment of the organ will permit: it is only in
> the cathedrals abroad that you can have these divine compositions properly

performed. In addition to the organ, there is a complete orchestra of all the instruments, without which the sublimities of these works can not be shown. I am informed that the posthumous Mass of Beethoven is attempted by the Bavarian choir.

From Warwick Street the company moved to the Chapel Royal and, after sitting through the service in Sir George Smart's organ loft, went to St Paul's to finish the day with evensong followed by dinner at the London Coffee-House. Besides Gardiner, those present were Thomas Attwood, George Cooper, and Samuel Wesley.[10]

Eight years later the music at Warwick Street was still praiseworthy. A caustic essay on 'English Cathedral Music' drew attention to the 'well-appointed vocal band' in the chapel, 'but let [the reader] wander to St Paul's, and he would encounter poverty and slovenliness, a meagre and inefficient choir, a careless performance – neither principal nor chorus, but a makeshift for both'.[11]

As the Novello family exercized much influence in the general field of English music, so too did the Wesleys, whose record in this respect begins with Samuel Wesley (1662–1735), sometime Rector of Epworth, in Lincolnshire. In 1694 he wrote an *Ode to St Cecilia* which, a hundred years later, was set to music by his grandson – also Samuel. The sons of the Rector of Epworth, Charles (1707–88) and John (1703–91) – the founders of Methodism – in different ways affected the character of sacred music. From John came expressions of philosophic piety and injunctions concerning propriety in the use of music in worship. One of these could well have belonged to a Papal *motu proprio*:

> Let the original simple, grave and devotional style be carefully preserved, which instead of drawing attention to singing and the singers, is so admirably calculated to draw off the attention from both, and to raise the soul to God only'.[12]

Charles Wesley effectively was the creator of modern popular hymnody. In the Preface to his own collection of hymns of 1849, F W Faber – across the sectarian divide – acknowledged the influence both of the Hymns of Wesley and the Olney Hymns of William Cowper 'among the English poor'.

Charles and Samuel – the two sons of Charles Wesley – in respect of music were both extremely gifted. Samuel was correctly described as an infant prodigy. His musicality, as executant, as composer, and as percipient scholar, was of a rare order. Of the early flowering of his creative talent there is ample evidence, not only in the records of others, but in his existing letters and other documents, and in his compositions. There was, however, a price to pay.

Samuel Wesley was neither the first nor the last eighteen-year-old to have experienced a spiritual crisis. In 1784 – to the distress of his family – it was common gossip that he had become a Catholic. Whether he had been baptized into the church is doubtful. None the less, as an act of faith he composed a *Missa de Spiritu Sancto* – for solo singers, chorus and orchestra – more ambitious than any Catholic music composed in England since the Reformation, and sent it, in a tin box, to Pope Pius VI, to whom it was fulsomely dedicated.

The Pope, in a letter to the vicar apostolic of the London district, James Talbot, acknowledged receipt of this unexpected tribute. What gave most pleasure to the Pope was a phrase in the covering letter he had received from Talbot, concerning the 'skill in religious controversy, in which you say, he excels, and the very good hopes you yourself entertain of him'.[13]

Throughout his life Wesley was subject to changes of mood, from boyish hilarity, across challenging perceptions of the comic, to clouded moods of emotional insecurity. He had sustained head injuries in a fall in his youth, which has been held responsible (without specific evidence) for many of his behavioural eccentricities. What is certain is that his emotional life – after separation from his wife, and in cohabitation with the lady who took her place – ran an uncertain course. At the same time he was accepted into a brilliant circle of friendship and distinction, of which the social centre was the lively household of Vincent Novello. Whether or not he became, in fact, a Catholic is less important than the fact that the music, which was his spiritual life, was music for the Catholic rite. For this, in post-Reformation England, music of comparable quality has rarely been written. Attracted at an early age to the sound of the music in the Portuguese Chapel Samuel once memorably said, 'If the Roman Doctrines were like the Roman *Music* we should have Heaven upon Earth'.[14]

Catholic music flowed from Wesley's pen across some forty years. Gregorian chant (as it was then understood) was a starting point, and he took account of the restrictions placed on a composer by the fact that the norm for a Catholic choir without trebles (as was generally the case) was not the familiar SATB arangement, but often a disposition of parts convenient for three or four men's voices – with one or two countertenors, tenor and bass. Gregorian chant was frequently treated as formally as in the *Missa in duplicibus* of 1789, or in the motet *Levate capita nostra* of 1798 (published in Novello's *Motets for the Morning Service*). In 1799 two especially fine works were written. One was a large-scale setting of Psalm 111 (*Confitebor tibi, Domine*). This is, perhaps, the only major work to have been published in modern times without ever having been previously publicly performed.[15] In the same year *Deus Majestatis*[16] for double choir and orchestra was written, to be followed in 1800 with *Exultate Deo* for five voice chorus and orchestra (or organ). The future of the last work, however, was not in the church for which it was intended, but in the Church of England, in which Wesley's son, Samuel Sebastian Wesley, wielded much influence.

In 1808 Wesley began seriously to consider his exploration of the works of J S Bach, in the propagation of whose music he was consistently supported on the one hand by Benjamin Jacob, organist of the Surrey (independent) Chapel, and on the other by Vincent Novello. 'Novello and myself', he wrote, 'were much in the habit of playing many of the fugues at the Chapel in South Street as voluntaries after the morning Service, as also Jacob did the same at the Surrey Chapel'.[17] Among those infected by this enthusiasm was Charles Butler, who wrote to Wesley on 7 October 1812:

> I have a note from Dr. Burney expressing the wish, that you and I would, as he calls it, 'mount his lofty apartment [in the Royal Hospital in Chelsea] next Sunday about 12 at Noon, and let him hear from you, a thorough Bach of the Great Sebastian's Golden Grain.[18]

Wesley held no official position in the musical profession. He gave lessons to support himself and his family. He gave lectures at the Royal Institution. Regarded as one of the best of organists, he frequently gave recitals in various parts of the country. At the centre of his life, however, was the music of Bach and of the Portuguese Embassy Chapel where he frequently deputized for Novello at the organ. He wrote his experiences into his letters, which were more often than not distinguished by a degree of humorous impiety.

In his Reminiscences Wesley wrote how 'Church music, Theatrical music and secular music in general (including concert music) each require a separate and appropriate style'. He studied the Italian masters of the 16th and 17th centuries, noticing that they 'took sundry pieces of Gregorian melody as subjects whereupon to model their most admirable specimens of counterpoint', and he paid particular respect to Palestrina, as in the Christmas antiphon *Hodie Christus natus est*.[19]

There is accordingly in Wesley's (mostly unknown) *oeuvre* a wide range of styles. Liturgically he made appropriate use of plainchant, and was dismayed when, in 1812, there was an antipathy towards Gregorian chant shown by some of the priests at the Embassy Chapel. In consequence of this feeling Wesley put aside his recently completed Mass in D (*Missa de angelis*), regretting the time which he had, he said, 'imprudently and incautiously sacrificed.' In the same year a typically acceptable classically-inclined setting of *Ave verum* was presented to the chapel singers.

At the other end of Wesley's expressional resource is a magnificent, powerfully expressive *Exultate Deo*,[20] with bold key contrasts.

Ex 8.

Hodie Christus natus est

Ex 9.

Ave verum

Ex. 10

Exultate Deo a, b, c

Of works of his later period the most eloquent example is the *Carmen Funèbre (Omnia Vanitas)* of 1827, of which it was said that 'the words were repeated to him by his father on his death-bed.[21] Of this and *Tu es sacerdos* Samuel's son, Samuel Sebastian Wesley, wrote in his 'A Few Words on Cathedral Music' of 1849:

> If a composer could have written as well as this when cathedral music was in such a poor condition as it was in his day, there is yet hope for church music.

Between church and chapel musicians contemporary with Wesley and Novello, there was frequent interchange of organ stools and ideas. Through their chapel commitments Novello and Wesley created a style which was recognizably 'Catholic' and influential. The challenge to Protestantism that was soon to be raised by the Tractarians was anticipated through a growing fascination with 'ancient music' on the part of musicians of the established church. William Russell, organist of the Foundling Hospital, composed a number of works for Catholic use, including a severe, contrapuntal, four-part Mass in C minor,[22] as well as motets in a more genial style. In 1808 Russell submitted his Exercise for the Bachelor of Music Degree at Oxford.[23] The required public performance took place at the music school on 26 January. Prefaced by a passionate sinfonia, this was a mature piece to match the classical vigour of Wesley's festal style.

Ex 11.

'Kyrie' of Mus B exercise

On 5 January 1827, Frederick Augustus, Duke of York, second son of George III, died. Although it was public knowledge that in 1825 he had voted against emancipation in the House of Lords he was charitably mourned in a sombre motet composed by John Goss (1800–1880), then organist of Chelsea New Church.[24].

Ex 12.

Requiem[25]

Notes

1   *The Downside Review*, 1, 1882 p 329. Morris was educated by Benedictines at Acton Burnell, Salop, admitted to minor orders in Wolverhampton by Bishop Milner, before entering Downside in 1814; 1832 vicar apostolic, South Africa and the Pacific.

2   Cowden-Clarke, Mary, *Musical Times*, 1862, vol 10 p 205.

3   GM Jan/June 1816, p 232; *Hebrew Melodies*, Lord Byron and Isaac Nathan (c 1790–1864).

4   *The Catholic Gentleman's Magazine*, 1818, p 573.

5   QMMR, 1819, p 210.

6   [Holmes, E], *A Musical Tour*, London 1828, p 68.

7   Farrell, op.cit., p 28.

8   *Mus. W.*, v, April 1836, p 47.

9   *The Catholic Penny Magazine*, Dublin, no 29, 1, 30 August, 1834.

10 Gardiner: I, pp 649–653; 'the musical performance at the Embassy Chapel was sometimes irreverently called 'the shilling opera'. George Cooper (1820–1876), sub-Organist, St Paul's Cathedral, organist and music master at Christ's Hospital.

11 'English Cathedral Music', *British and Foreign Review*, XVII, 1844, pp 115–116'.

12 Barrett, Philip, *A Digest of the Methodist Conference 1744–1826*, pp 22–23; no 4 of regulations from the 'excellent rules drawn up by our venerable Father in the gospel, Mr. Wesley, in respect to singing'.

13 Lightwood, James T, *Samuel Wesley Musican*, London 1937, pp 66–67.

14 Wesley to Benjamin Jacob, 5 November 1809; see *The Bach Letters of Samuel Wesley*, ed Elisha Wesley, Introduction by Percy M Young, Da Capo, New York 1981.

15 *Confitebor* see *Mus Brit* XLI.

16 RCM MS 550.

17 BM Add MS 27593, f 51.

18 BM Add MS 11729, f 36.

19 BM Add MS 35001, f 92.

20 BM Add MS 17711, f 26–27.

21 BM Add MS 35003, no 24; see *Mus W*, VII, nos LXXXIII, IV, VI, Oct 13, 20; Nov 3, pp 79, 81, 113, 1837.

22 RCM MS 550.

23 Bodleian Music School ex C 241.

24 A former chorister of the Chapel Royal, Goss became organist of St Paul's Cathedral in 1838.

25 BM Add MS Add 31821.

3 Parochial Music: London and the North

London

Early in the nineteenth century the fact of Roman Catholicism assuming – if not acceptance – at least a more positive national significance, was demonstrated by two notable, if melancholy, events. On 5 November 1817 the Princess Charlotte Augusta – married only in the previous year to Prince Leopold, of Saxe-Coburg – died in childbirth. A general sense of grief at the death of this much loved, seventeen-year-old daughter of George IV was given expression in contrasting manner:

> At the catholic chapels, high mass was celebrated in the most solemn manner, particularly at the Portuguese ambassador's, where the music was of the sublimest kind'.[1]

Vincent Novello paid a personal tribute to the Princess in setting to music a poem by his friend Leigh Hunt – 'His departed love to Prince Leopold'. On 19 November the funeral took place at St George's Chapel, Windsor Castle. On the following night there was a public display of mourning in the Royal Opera House, Covent Garden.

> The pillars [in the house] were entwined with bands of black cloth, which were secured at the capitals by knots of white ribbons ... the box usually occupied by Princess Charlotte was hung with black. Music appropriate to the occasion consisted chiefly of Mozart's Requiem, one of the noblest efforts of human genius, the sublime Funeral Anthem of Handel, and the last Act of the Messiah, with the Dead March in Saul, and a few sacred songs intermixed.[2]

The music was selected, and directed, by Sir George Smart (organist of the Chapel Royal), who had often arranged concerts for the Princess.[3]

Ten years later Smart was again concerned with a commemorative performance of Mozart's Requiem. In February 1826, at Smart's invitation,

Carl Maria von Weber came from Dresden to London for the first performance of *Oberon* – which he was to conduct – at Covent Garden. For some months he lived in Smart's house while he rehearsed the opera and fulfilled a number of social and musical engagements. Incurably ill before he left Dresden, his health so deteriorated that towards the end of May – when he should have returned to Germany – it was clear that he was in no way fit to do so. On the morning of 5 June he was found to have died during the night.

Admired as a musician in England, in Saxony Weber was also esteemed as a patriot, who through his music extended patriotism. On behalf of the musicians of London, a delegation approached the priests of St Mary's Chapel, Moorfields, to ask that the valediction to Weber – a Catholic and the composer of three settings of the Mass – should be by way of a public funeral at which Mozart's Requiem would be performed. Weber – his father being brother to Mozart's wife Constanze – was a nephew of the composer.

On Friday 24 April, Weber's body was taken from Smart's house in Bedford Square in a solemn procession to Moorfields. The hearse, drawn by six horses, was followed by twenty coaches of friends and admirers. At the chapel were the best orchestral players from Covent Garden and the Philharmonic Society, led by Francois Cramer; celebrated solo singers – the Misses Cubitt, Povey, Betts, Andrews and Farrar, and Messrs Braham, Pyne, Evans, Pinto, and Phillips – 'assisted by the Ladies and Gentlemen of the Choir of the Catholic Chapel and a chorus of 36 singers'. John Terrail, the usual organist,[4] surrendered his place to Thomas Attwood, organist of St Paul's Cathedral.[5] As the body was lowered into the vault Handel's 'Dead March' from *Saul* was played.

Five years later, on 14 January 1831, a Requiem for the lately deceased Pius VIII – whose pontificate had lasted for less than two years – took place at Moorfields. 'A Solemn Dirge . . .' was intoned in plain Gregorian chant by the clergy, without the usual accompaniments of organ and choir.

Vincent Novello was briefly connected with St Mary's Moorfields, where, during his late period as organist – between 1841 and 1843 – he was on one occasion extraordinarily interrupted:

> At a recent celebration of Mass in the metropolitan Catholic chapel Moorfields, in consequence of some dispute between the choir and Mr. V. Novello, the organist, the latter left the organ-loft abruptly, at the moment of commencing the service, taking with him the organ-score; and, in consequence, Haydn's fine Mass, No. 2, which is particularly full in the accompaniment, was performed by the voices alone, counting out the bars and other rests devoted to the symphonies and instrumental portions of the composition. Whether these extraordinary 'new effects' were admirable or appropriate, we are not informed; but it is certain they were deemed worthy

of imitation, like other musical monstrosities; for Mr. Lejeune, the organist of the London Road chapel, St. George's Fields, on a subsequent Sunday, indulged the congregation with a similar piece of heresy.[6]

By this time the need for a new and larger chapel in Southwark, to serve a continually increasing and indigent Catholic community, mostly of Irish immigrants, was urgent. As was frequently the case in such circumstances, it was the clergy who were expected to act. James Talbot – who succeeded Richard Challoner as vicar apostolic in 1786 – approved the use for the time being of a modest building in Bandyleg Walk to serve as chapel. Thomas Walsh, a Douai-trained priest, was appointed to take charge of the congregation, for some time being assisted by an American priest, Father John Thayer. Within two years, the temporary chapel having become inadequate to the needs of the congregation, the decision was taken to build in its place one that was worthy of its function.

On 21 January 1793, soon after the melancholy event of the execution of Louis xvi of France had taken place, a Requiem was sung in commemoration in the old Mass House. In March a 'large and grand chapel'[7] in the London Road was ready for occupation, and on St Patrick's Day the vicar apostolic, Bishop Doyle, pontificated at high mass. The new chapel was dedicated to St George. In 1801 James Bramston (in due course also to become vicar apostolic) came to the chapel. Here he served the Southwark Mission for 23 years. From 1817 until 1820, and then again from 1839 for ten productive years, the organist was Henry George Nixon, son-in-law of John Danby.[8]

For a period in the late 1830s the music at St George's was much noticed by the *Musical World*, which was in general favourably disposed to the best equipped Catholic chapels. Regarding the morning service on Easter Day in 1837 and the performance of Haydn's Mass No 6 [*Harmonie-Messe*], its contributor wrote:

> . . . with due allowance for the present condition of the choir, it was got through very effectively. The soloist was Mrs Fitzwilliam . . . Mr. Nixon's clever and spirited Offertorium in E, 'Victime Paschale' was well sung (we know not by whom), though it would have lost nothing by a little more steadiness in the notes.

> . . . Our chapel singers are much neglected by the public, and consequently the press. How is this? Is it because they are above the prevailing taste for florid vulgarity and noise?[9]

In 1837 St George's also served as the chapel of the diplomatic mission of the newly established Kingdom of Belgium. For a time the music was entrusted to a brilliant young German, a pupil of Weber, who was beginning to establish himself as opera composer and conductor in London.

At the Vespers last Sunday evening . . . the usual Gregorian service, which has of late been so undeservedly neglected, was finely performed by a full choir. Miss Clara Novello sang several solos, and was well supported by the choir. Mr. Benedict, the organist to the chapel, presided.[10]

We are pleased to hear that means are taking to secure an equally efficient performance of the Vespers once a month. The collection upon the present occasion (which was large) is to be appropriated to the fund for building the new church.[11]

For the anniversary of the consecration of the chapel in November, the choir – assisted by Miss Betts, Mrs Serle, Messrs Wilson, Dobson, Giubilei, and others – sang selections from the Masses of Haydn and Mozart. In respect of the 'Et incarnatus' from Mozart No 12 the correspondent of the *Musical World* was ecstatic: 'As we have never heard this perfectly divine movement better sung, so have we rarely heard a service better selected, or more equally performed.'[12]

It was in St George's in 1841 that, under Nixon, the first performance in England was given of Rossini's *Stabat Mater*. Novello's third daughter, Cecilia, actress as well as singer, was the soprano soloist.

Father Thomas Boyle, parish priest since 1829, immediately began to plan towards a building worthy of the metropolitan status St George's was to adopt. It having been decided to engage Augustus Welby Northmore Pugin as architect, work began in 1840. For him this was his first great opportunity to demonstrate the moral purpose behind his exclusive use of Gothic style. By this means Catholicism was reunited with its mediaeval origins. When finished the building, with the dimensions of a cathedral, was the finest Catholic church in London. A nave of eight huge bays, flanked by aisles furnished with chapels, and an impressively raised sanctuary, it presented a new magnificence to the people living around and was the centre of Catholic life in London until the opening of Westminster Cathedral fifty years later.[13]

On 4 July 1848, the new St George's was consecrated by Thomas Walsh, vicar apostolic of the Midland District, in the presence of the other seven vicars apostolic. Nixon presided at the organ. The choir consisted of fifty voices – including a substantial group of boys from different Catholic schools of the metropolis, and a number of Italian opera singers. Among these were Antonio Tamburini, Giovanni Mario, and Conte di Candia – the most popular tenor of his day. The choirmaster and organist – who held his post from 1848 to 1874 – was Meyer Lutz.[14] Music for the occasion was strongly German-Austrian: for the Mass, by Hummel and Droboisch, for the introit, 'Haec Dies' by Ett, and for the offertory, 'Lauda Sion' by Michael Haydn.[15]

Two years after its consecration, St George's became a focus for national interest and concern. On 24 September 1850 Pope Pius IX issued an apostolic letter, announcing the establishment of a Catholic hierarchy in England. On the next day Nicholas Wiseman, having been created cardinal, promptly issued a 'Pastoral appointed to be read . . . in the Archdiocese of Westminster and the Diocese of Southwark', which was followed by a series of three explanatory lectures delivered in St George's. Here in December Wiseman was spectacularly enthroned. After the reception of the cardinal at the western porch, the procession of clergy prepared to enter the church:

> The organ, which up to this hour had played a soft monotonous soothing air, suddenly pealed forth, in tones that rolled and echoed through every vaulted arch of the building, the triumphant notes of the antiphon, 'Ecce Sacerdos Magnus', followed by the Hallelujah chorus from Beethoven's *Mount of Olives*.[16]

Wiseman's Pastoral was not acceptable to the Protestant majority in England. Many Catholics, including a number of the influential laity, disliking the triumphal tone of the message, were alarmed that disorder could ensue. Wiseman, it was said, had lived too long away from England to appreciate adequately the national temper in the matter. For the benefit of potential opponents to the new authority allowed to the Roman Catholics, a not entirely objective book in the form of an extended horror story – *The Popes: an Historical Summary*, by G H F Wilks MD – was published in 1851. In August of that year Parliament passed an 'Ecclesiastical Titles Assumption Act' (repealed by Gladstone in 1872) by which a fine of £100 was to be paid by anyone assuming such a title. Apart from the fact that this was never invoked, it should be noted that exactly the same legislation had been detailed in section XXIV of the Bill published in 1829.

In 1836 James Gattie had called attention to the recent increase of Catholic places of worship, and to opportunities offered for musical experience:

> the public, it seems, have at length discovered that Mozart is still Mozart, wherever he is to be found; and that the music of Haydn loses nothing of its sweetness by being heard even at a Papist chapel.[17]

Expressing surprise that the Catholic clergy did not think of turning the choirs into sources of revenue, instead of allowing them to stay as they were – a drain on their finances – Gattie drew attention to 'the just claims of these places to be considered among the most efficient schools of musical instruction the country at present possesses'. There was also, he noted, a large number of reputable soloists whose musical education was owed to the best of the Catholic choirs.

One church conspicuous for ambitious musical performances was St Mary's Chapel, Chelsea. Here Joseph Warren, a musician of all-round ability, and a significant figure among the second generation of Catholic church musicians, had been appointed organist in 1834. He was ambitious, but he could not have realized his aims within the opportunities available to a minor church musician. However, he made the most of those occasions where music was particularly important. He also gained some credit for his educational activity.

In February 1837 *The Musical World* commented on

> a class of singers, chiefly young girls, connected with some of the smaller Catholic chapels. It is pleasant to behold the sagacity and perseverance with which these fair votaries of music, whose parents have no money to spend upon masters, will avail themselves of the facilities of these places . . . . Two of the most promising of these fair students of Haydn and Mozart are to be heard at St. Mary's Chapel, Chelsea, and that in Virginia-street [East Smithfield]. Miss Schluster of the former chapel has a superior voice of good quality; her intonation is correct, and her style good. Miss Bassano of the chapel in Virginia-street, has a soprano voice of great compass; she sings very well in tune, and there is a simplicity and musician-like ease in her style, from which, with perseverance, much might be expected.[18]

On 15 October of that year, after several months of closure on account of repair work, the reopening of St Mary's was celebrated by the first English performance of Weber's First Mass in G.[19] For Joseph Warren there was an equally important occasion on 26 November – the annual day for collections to be given to the schools fund. On this day his Mass in D was given its first performance, for which Warren assembled a professional quartet of solo singers. The soprano was Miss Beer, described as 'no novice in the art of singing', and with a voice 'powerful enough to fill a theatre'. Miss Pickersgill, the contralto, sang the Benedictus 'most charmingly'. The tenor, Mr Farrier, a pupil of Giovanni Battista Rubini, was a member of the Spanish Embassy choir and sang 'with much truth'. Collet Dobson, bass, 'acquitted himself admirably'.[20]

To the general public Warren's position at St Mary's suggested professional respectability. Although the salary was small (as were all such posts at the time) it gave him a position from which to claim pupils. More importantly, it enabled him to engage in his study of old music. In this respect he was a pioneer musicologist, who published an edition of John Hilton's *Ayres, or Fa la las* (1627) for the Musical Antiquarian Society in 1844, and an edition of William Boyce's *Cathedral Music* in 1848. Warren published many articles and edited much music for various publishers.[21] At one point in his career it seems that Warren suffered considerable mental strain. In 1845 and 1846 he was troubled with family problems and at one point he was disturbed by rumours concerning his private life that seemed to be circulated among certain people at his church. In 1846 he was received into the Catholic Church.[22]

The character of Catholic church music in London was largely determined by the fact that for a missionary church beset with political and financial problems, and served by priests with varying experience but few with knowledge of music, there were other priorities. The chief need was for schools and churches. For the most part music was not high on the list of the considerations of a parish priest, so that the fact that organists – while required to provide acceptable music – might need to make a living was seldom recognized. Singers could easily be engaged on a casual basis, and for a fee there were many immigrant professionals from the opera houses who were willing to assist, at least on special occasions. Among the new chapels that of St Aloysius, Somers Town, gained a reputation for musical excellence, but here there were special circumstances, for Vincent Novello's son, Alfred, led the choir, of which his sister Mary and her husband, Charles Cowden-Clarke, were enthusiastic members.[23]

The North

The Act of 1791, 'to relieve, upon condition and under certain restrictions persons called protesting Catholic Dissenters, to which papists, or, persons protesting the popish religion, are by law subject', within limits, gave both to Catholic worship and education a degree of independence. It therefore became possible, for the first time since the Reformation, to begin to establish centres for the training of priests in England.

In the northern counties there were families of standing who, living remotely, far from London, had been constant in religion across the centuries. Among them were those who had often been ready to offer safe haven to seminarians sent from European houses to join the English mission. In the aftermath of the French Revolution, and of war between England and France, and the enforced closure of Douai and other European institutions, many priests and students were obliged to return to England. There was then need for new schools and seminaries to replace those that had educated the sons of many Catholic families, and priests for more than two hundred years.

A number of students and professors with northern antecedents, evacuated from Douai, were taken into temporary accommodation in Co Durham, under the authority of William Gibson, vicar apostolic of the Northern District, who from 1781 to 1790 had been President of Douai. After some years he was able to purchase from Sir Edward Smythe – a Catholic landowner – a site at Ushaw, near Durham City. Here on 19 July

1808 the first part of an ambitious building designed by James Taylor – the architect of Moorfields – was ready for occupation by 47 students and five professors.

In its early days Ushaw was led by Thomas Eyre, President, and John Lingard, vice president. The second president, John Gillow, like Lingard, was a former Douai student. In 1791 he had been assigned to the mission in York (where he remained for twenty years) before succeeding to Eyre at Ushaw. Under him the college prospered, and his own authority grew. He became a trusted adviser to the vicars apostolic during the period leading to the Toleration Act of 1829. During the first half of the nineteenth century the college consistently increased its numbers. On the one hand were students for the priesthood, needed for new parishes in the expanding northern industrial towns; on the other, boys of Catholic families in quest of a good general education, some of whom would also ultimately seek the priesthood.

An approving notice of music at Ushaw during the early 1830s is contained in a letter from James Standen, a former student, to Joseph Brown, Rector of St Alban's College, Valladolid. Standen was writing under the impression of his first visit to Burgos Cathedral:

> You have indeed fine music at Ushaw and fine ceremonies and fine processions, but, until you have heard Catholic music, seen Catholic ceremonies and followed Catholic processions, you can form no idea of the great effect they are capable of producing.[24]

The fine music was largely due to the personal interest and energy of Charles Newsham, a former student of Ushaw, sometime prefect of studies, choirmaster, and vice president, who became president in 1837. As such he exercised considerable influence in the general development of the college. During his period of office a collection of manuscript copies of music – almost entirely liturgical – was brought to Ushaw from Rome. One item of unusual interest in this collection is a Te Deum setting in four parts, by Fortunato Santini, Music Librarian of the Vatican. The work is inscribed *Per il desideratissimo e felicissimo Ritorno Della Santita di N.S. Pio Papa IX. Nella sua S. Sede, dedico al Rev. D. Carlo Newsham Rettore del Collegio di S. Cuthberto di Ushaw.*[25]

Other works included the Lamentations of Palestrina associated with the Holy Week ceremonies in the Sistine Chapel and Masses by Francisco Anerio, Padre D Filippo Borsi, and Giovanni [Battista] Casali. Of these works of Casali, the second is marked 'arranged by Dr. Crookall in G Major', the third ('The score of this has unaccountably been lost') by J Richardson, and the fifth by Dr Crookall. There are numerous motets, some by Palestrina, but most by eighteenth century Roman and Neapolitan composers of church music, including Niccolo Pasquali, Pasquale Anfossi,

Giovanni Cavi, Giovanni Battista Casali, Francesco Durante, and Giuseppe Jannacconi. There is also a separate copy of Henry Harrington's plangent 'Prayer of Mary Queen of Scots before her execution'.

A miscellaneous volume with motets by various Italian composers also contains works by Matthew Peter King,[26] Samuel Webbe junior, and the Reverend William Green D D and the Reverend Roland Davies.[27] English Catholic composers in former times learned how to make the best of meagre resources. Much of this music, comfortable to sing, is sentimentally attractive to the ear. The idiom was infectious, and the texture agreeable to unpretentious singers.

Among former students of Ushaw, the most celebrated was Nicholas Wiseman, who neither forgot the pleasure he received from music during his student years nor failed to acknowledge a debt of gratitude to Newsham. On the occasion of the jubilee of the college, in July 1858, a new college ode, 'written and dedicated to the Students of St. Cuthbert's College by His Eminence Cardinal Wiseman', set to music by John Richardson, was performed for the first time.

In 1742 Thomas Daniel, the first priest of a new mission in York, established himself, not far from the Minster, in a house in Little Blake Street. Eighteen years later, in the same street, a public place of worship [St Wilfrid's] was opened, and this was replaced, during the pastorate of Rev John Gillow, by public subscription, with

> ... a handsome brick building of modern architecture about 74 feet in length, 44 feet broad, and 30 feet in height, and capable of containing 700 persons. It comprises a very large gallery, neatly fitted up, also an organ gallery or loft, with other requisite appendages. Attached to the chapel, are likewise convenient apartments for the residence of the officiating pastor.[28]

From 1811 to 1842 the priest of the Mission was Rev Benedict Rayment, second son of Thomas Rayment of Worcester.[29] Educated at Douai, Rayment ministered in Flanders during the French Revolution. From the beginning of his pastorate in York music became increasingly important. An organ, said to have carried the label of 'James Davis, organ builder [of Lancashire]',[30] was installed at an early date, and the first organist was a singing teacher, Frederick Hill.[31]

A happy combination of wealth and cultural energy that distinguished some among the Catholic gentry brought about a remarkable, and encouraging, event on the last Tuesday in May, 1816,

> when high mass was celebrated at the Catholic Chapel in Blake-street, a spectacle which has not been exhibited in York, with so great a degree of splendor, during the last three hundred years.

The celebrant, Matthew Newsham, was chaplain to the Constable

Maxwell family at Everingham, where a large classical chapel was built during the latter part of the eighteeth century.

> Miss Danby, several gentlemen amateurs of this city, and the choristers of the Cathedral, generously lent their aid on this interesting occasion: and we cannot say too much in praise of the performance of each; Mr. James Atkinson, was leader of the band – Mr. Camidge, jun. presided at the organ: and Gen. Bosville on the Violincello [*sic*].

The performance, 'crowded by members of every religious persuasion', lasted from 11.30 to 1.30 pm. Father Rayment, in preaching the Charity Sermon, distinguished himself

> by the liberality of sentiment which he expressed towards those of every other religious persuasion, [he] excited a congenial feeling and good will towards the Roman Catholics, and proved himself on this, as on other occasions, the able advocate of unprotected innocence . . . and the Charity School, for which the collection was taken, benefited to the extent of £70.[32]

Matthew Camidge had succeeded his father as organist of York Minster in 1803, to be followed by his son some forty years later. He remained a good friend to the Catholics. On at least one occasion, in 1821, he played at 'High Mass' in St Wilfrid's,

> when exquisite passages from Haydn, Beethoven, Handel and Cherubini were rendered and in addition to the choir, Mrs. George, Mr. Erskine and Mr Bradley Lang. Mr. Erskine was a principal performer on the oboe at the concerts given by Dr. Camidge. It was not uncommon for Dr. Camidge to play the organ at St. Wilfrid's when any special service was given.[33]

Frederick Hill's successor as organist of St Wilfrid's was John Robinson, a music dealer, an excellent clarinettist, and one of the leading musicians in the city, who enjoyed a reputation that was not only local. Vincent Novello had such confidence in him that he sent his son [Joseph] Alfred to York to learn from Robinson the business of music-selling. Alfred, indentured for five years on 17 May 1824, soon became a member of the choir of St Wilfrid's and lodged with its principal soprano, Miss Betsy Hill. In due course Miss Hill was to invest a considerable sum of money in his publishing business.[34]

In 1827 the nine-year-old Clara Novello was sent to join her brother in York, to be taught by Robinson, and to follow Miss Hill's example. One Sunday, in the absence of the soprano soloist, claiming to know by heart the Haydn and Mozart items set for the day, Clara precociously offered herself as substitute and – it appears – vindicated her claim.

As teacher, Robinson followed conservative principles as painfully described by Clara:

> He gave me rare and short detested lessons on the pianoforte, hitting my knuckles with a big red pencil he marked fingerings with. I was left for hours

daily before the pianoforte, in a room seldom used, and soon I substituted for Cramer's Exercises any vocal music I could run off with from the shelves, and thus I learnt to read and decipher music, never reflecting that my delinquency would be discovered by my voice instead of my fingers being hard at work.[35]

In September 1828 Vincent Novello, having recently announced his intention of undertaking an edition of Purcell's church music, came to York at the time of the York Festival to copy Purcell manuscripts in the Minster Library. In one day he is said to have transcribed the G minor evening service and four anthems, which, but for his industry, would have been lost in the great fire of 2 February 1829.[36] Since Robinson's time as organist there had remained in St Wilfrid's Church thirteen choirbooks. Of these, eleven contain familiar publications of Vincent Novello. A twelfth volume is '*A Collection of Sacred Music Calculated for the use of Small Choirs* . . . humbly Inscribed to the Roman Catholic/Prelates of Scotland/ by/The Revd G.G. (price for subscribers 12/6/Engraved & Printed by Waller & Anderson to be had by applying to any Catholic Clergy of Scotland.' The thirteenth volume, a manuscript collection, contains a small and charming motet, idiomatically apt to Catholic performance, by the son or (probably) grandson of Charles Avison of Newcastle. All three Avisons were organists of St Nicholas's Church in the city.

Ex. 13

O Jesu dulcis

There are also works by Hummel, Novello, and Samuel Webbe, as well as Maurice Greene's anthem 'Behold I bring you glad tidings'. The volume is labelled: 'Webbe's Mass / in B ♭ / Arranged for / 4 Voices / by / John Robinson 1832'. Several of Novello's masses were arranged by him for his purposes at St Wilfrid's, while Samuel Webbe's Mass in C would seem to have been performed when the church was opened.

In 1840 Robinson was succeeded at St Wilfrid's by George Hopkinson, a former chorister at the Minster and a pupil of Camidge under whom – apparently with the encouragement of Bishop John Briggs –

Masses by Mozart, Weber, Cherubini, Haydn and others were in regular use and at a concert given in April 1860 the principal soloists were Mrs

Willem and [Miss] Alice Watson [who] with an orchestra gathered from York and Leeds and the St Wilfrid's Choir rendered Haydn's No.6 Mass under the conductorship of Mr. Geo. Hopkinson.[37]

In the meantime in the greater manufacturing towns in the northern counties Catholicism was making dramatic progress. This was especially the case in Leeds. Here, at the end of the eighteenth century, a Dominican mission supported by the Catholic families of the county had established St Mary's chapel. With increasing opportunities for employment great numbers of Irish Catholics flooded into the town, as a result of which the existing chapel became inadequate. In July 1832 a new chapel, dedicated to St Patrick, was consecrated when the inescapable 'Twelfth Mass' of Mozart was sung. At this time it was decided to replace St Mary's chapel. The commission was given to a local architect, John Child, who in a true Gothic spirit crowned the new chapel with a spire. At the time of its opening in 1838, in honour of two ladies who were principal benefactors, the dedication was changed to St Anne, which, with Pugin's celebrated reredos of 1842, was carried forward into the successor building, the cathedral of 1904.

In preparation for his *A Tour through England and Wales* Daniel Defoe travelled from York to Durham. By his account, Catholics in Durham, at the begining of the eighteenth century, enjoyed the benefit of a society exceptionally endowed with the spirit of tolerance.

> The town is well built, but old, full of Roman Catholicks, who live peaceably and disturb no body, and no body them; for we being there on holiday, saw them going as publicly to mass as the Dissenters did on other days to their meeting-house.[38]

Defoe's description was remarkably accurate, for there had been Mass houses in and around Durham throughout recusant times. On this account the district called Elvet had sometimes been known as 'Popish Elvet'. Father Thomas Pearson, a Jesuit, was active in Durham from before 1688 until his death in 1732 and he had built a chapel and school at Old Elvet. The secular clergy were also active and had a chapel and clergy house at 33 Old Elvet.[39]

In 1824 Fr William Croskell (1767–1838), a Lancashire man and an alumnus of Douai, was appointed by Thomas Smith, vicar apostolic of the Northern District, to the parish of Elvet, with instruction to replace two inconveniently small chapels with one better building. The architect appointed was Ignatius Bonomi, whose father, Joseph, had come to England in 1767 at the invitation of the Adam brothers, through whom he had worked for the northern Lambton family.[40] The younger Bonomi settled in Durham where he was responsible for the Assize Court and the prison. Well respected generally in the north (he had taught John Child of

Leeds) he was commissioned to design the new chapel in Durham. A 'neat stone structure, in the Gothic style', dedicated to St Cuthbert, it was opened on 1 May 1827.

> ... High Mass was performed by the rev. Dr. Thomas Smith, Bishop of Bolino, and vicar apostolic of the northern district, the rev. Thomas Gillow, of North Shields, and others, an appropriate sermon was delivered by the Rev. James Wheeler. A band of about 15 musicians from Madame Tussaud's exhibition and theatre, executed one of Mozart's grand masses with great effect.[41]

The choir for the occasion was from Ushaw College. The instrumentalists, belonging to Madame Tussaud's touring company, were at the time happily stationed in Durham. Employing a circus band for the ceremony was perhaps stretching rather far the liberality of Pope Gregory XIV in respect of the use of instruments to accompany sacred music. In London, however, the hiring of professional musicians had been long established, and that (unless imported opera singers) they were normally non-Catholics was condoned on the grounds that the revenue they could bring in – often from non-Catholics – was a useful source for the sustentation of priests in poor parishes. The practice aroused some opposition when, in the galleries erected for their convenience and screened from the congregation behind curtains, talkative singers disturbed the proceedings below.

Music prospered in St Cuthbert's during the time of Croskell's successor, William Fletcher (d.1856). An organ was obtained from the London builder J C Bishop,[42] and an organist and choirmaster hired, whose organ-book together with the part-books for the singers served choristers for many years.[43]

> The choir developed a very wide reputation. They made full use of the compositions of the two Samuel Webbes, father and son, but the early books contain the names of Mozart, Haydn, Tallis (a chant for the Athanasian Creed) and a host of lesser known contemporary musicians – together with a few pieces of Gregorian chant.[44]

A stern discipline obtained. There were weekly practices; none but choristers were permitted to be in the choir-loft at any time; talking was forbidden, in order to 'promote good example and to exhibit due respect for the house of God'. Pieces to be sung should be approved by the chaplain and not changed without his authority.

Moreover, the obligations continued,

> To preserve unanimity and attention in the sacred duty of chanting the divine praises, each member of the choir must strictly and solely attend to his [and her?] own department and not interfere with that of another.[45]

St Cuthbert's was remarkable in England in being associated with the Cecilian movement. This had come into existence, at least in part, in consequence of the restatement of the principles concerning propriety in respect of the use of liturgical music by Popes Leo XII in 1824 and Pius VIII in 1830. In France and Germany this gave rise to a determination to reconstitute a unity between music and liturgy that should have a higher degree of authority than was general in the middle years of the nineteenth century. Obedience to tradition required the strict use of Gregorian chant and *a capella* works. At St Cuthbert's the journals of the St Cecilia Society were occasionally acquired, and the choir bravely attempted masses by Palestrina and those in polyphonic idiom by Franz Xavier Witt – one of the founders of the Cecilian movement. But however zealous were those in St Cuthbert's whose determination led them to require the 'traditional' music of the church, the men and women in the congregation resisted the imposition of Gregorian chant and Palestrina, and returned with relish to the familiarities of Mozart and Haydn et al. In this respect the parish of St Cuthbert, Durham, was not unique.

Notes

1   *The Orthodox Journal and Catholic Monthly Intelligencer*, vol v, 1817, p 448; C I Latrobe, *Selection of Sacred Music* (1806) ded. to Princess Charlotte.

2   Cutting from London newspaper, Barber Institute, Birmingham, ML46M.

3   On 18 September 1813 John Spencer reported a conversation between Princess Charlotte and Smart: 'Spencer: "I think your Royal Highness said you were acquainted with Sir George Smart." Princess: "Oh! Yes! I know him very well, and like him very much, he is such an excellent musician." (BL, Add MS 41777).

4   John Terrail, an excellent counter-tenor, was a member of the Madrigal Society and the Catch and Glee Club.

5   Thomas Attwood (1765–1838), studied with Mozart in Vienna 1785–7; organist of St Paul's Cathedral, 1796–1838.

6   *Mus W* New Series XVI, CLXXXIV, 8 July, 1841, p 46.

7   The architect was James Taylor who was also responsible for Ushaw College, Durham; see p 38.

8   Henry George Nixon (1796–1849): 1817–1820, organist, St George's Chapel (Cathedral); 1820–36, of the Bavarian Embassy Chapel; 1836–39, of St Andrew's Chapel, Glasgow; 1839, St George's Cathedral. Died during cholera epidemic of 1849. 1818 married Caroline Melissa Danby, daughter of John Danby. Their daughter Caroline Frances became organist of St Patrick's Chapel, Soho.

9   *Mus W* v, LIII, 17 March 1837, p 47.

10 Julius Benedict (1804–1885), born Germany, pupil of Weber; settled in England in 1835, conductor of opera and principal Music Festivals; prolific composer of opera and oratorio; naturalized British citizen, knighted in 1871.

11 *Mus W*, v, LXIV, 2 June 1837, p 191.

12 *Mus W* VII, LXXXVII, 10 Nov 1837, p 141.

13 The only parts of St George's Cathedral surviving the air-raids of 1941 were the outer walls, the tomb of the founder priest (later provost), Thomas Doyle (1797–1879), and the Knill and Petre chapels. In the subsequent restoration a clerestory was raised above the nave walls, enhancing Pugin's original design.

14 Wilhelm Meyer Lutz, German organist, composer, settled in England after 1848, successively Organist St Chad's, Birmingham, St Anne's, Leeds, St George's, London 1848–74.

15 *The Illustrated London News*, no 326, xiii, 15 July 1848, p 22. For a detailed account of the opening of the cathedral and the induction of Wiseman, see *The Great Link* (Southwark), pp 128f, 189f.

16 *AR*, 1850, p 149.

17 *Mus W*, iii , xxxiv, Nov 4 1836, p 113.

18 *Mus W*, iv, xlvii, 3 Feb [1837], p 111.

19 Ibid., vii, lxxxiv, 20 Oct 1837, p 95.

20 Ibid. xc, vii, 1 Dec p 191.

21 Edited many works for Robert Cocks, including Beethoven's *Mount of Olives*, Spohr's *Violin School*, and Rinck's *Organ Works* etc; for description of his library see *Music at Auction: Puttick and Simpson (of London), 1794–1971*, ed James Cooper, Detroit, 1988.

22 Letter of 30 August 1846, from his friend John Bishop, organist of the Catholic church in Cheltenham: 'I have just heard *with the deepest conceivable regret* that you have been admitted into the Roman Catholic church, you having been *confirmed* lately by the proper authorities'.

23 Cowden-Clarke, op cit, 20 Oct 1837, pp 112–113.

24 M E Williams, St Alban's College, Valladolid, London 1986, p 142.

25 In 1848 Italian aspirations for national unity led to the abdication of Pius ix from his secular territory temporarily to take refuge at Gaeta; he returned under the protection of France and Austria in 1850.

26 Matthew Peter King, composer of glees, part-songs, popular operas and elementary textbooks.

27 Rev Rowland Davies, organist, said to have taken part in the Coronation Service of George iii; trained for priesthood at Douai, to which he returned periodically after assuming pastoral duties in England; chaplain at Bavarian Embassy 1785; Mawhood, p 13; see Chapter 1, music example 3a.

28 Hargrove, William, *History and Description of the Ancient City of York*, 1818, p 473.

29 Register of Burials in the Parish of St Nicholas . . ., Worcester: John Rayment, aet.93, 18 September 1851; elder brother of Benedict Rayment.

30 Communication from Mr Dominic Minskip.

31 Communication from Mr N Page; the first organ was removed to the new church of St Wilfrid in 1864.

32 *The York Herald*, 1 June 1816, quoted in *Orthodox Journal*, 1816, p 252.

33 Hargrove, ibid.

34 Hurd, M, *Vincent Novello and Company*, London 1981, pp 28–29.

35 Cowden-Clarke, Mary, *The Life and Labours of Vincent Novello*, London 1864, p 2.

36 Cowden-Clarke, Mary, 'The Life and labours of Vincent Novello', *Mus T*, 1862, p 188.

37 Knowles, J[ohn] W[ard], *Notes on the organists, clerks, and quires in York churches since the Reformation*, 1924, MS Y942.7411, York Central Library.

38   Defoe, Daniel, *A Tour through England and Wales*, J M Dent, London 1928 (1939), 2 vols, II, pp 248–9.
39   Tweedy, J M et al. 1827–1977, *St Cuthbert's: a Paper prepared by a Parish History Group*, Durham [1977].
40   Bonomi senior, see Jane Austen, *Sense and Sensibility*, (1797–1811), XXXVI: Robert Ferrars, 'Lord Courtland came to me the other day on purpose to ask my advice, and laid before me three different plans of Bonomi's'. *Cath Mag* II,1833, p 116.
41   *Catholic Miscellany*, July 1827, Tweedy.
42   Bishop's Order Book, 4.11.1, Tweedy.
43   Choirbooks now in the Library of Ushaw College.
44   Tweedy.
45   Ibid.

4 The Midland District

St Mary's College, Oscott

Since the seventeenth century Catholicism had been cautiously maintained in the Midland District in a secluded country property at Oscott kept for the use of a priest. The first to live here was Andrew Bromwich who, having undergone many trials during the troubled days of the seventeenth century, came to familiar country where he died in 1703. John Talbot Stonor, vicar apostolic of the Midland District during the first half of the eighteenth century, had another house built at Oscott as a residence for his successors. This was as a precaution against the possibility of a property on the Chillington estate in Staffordshire, traditionally assigned to the vicars, becoming unavailable. A change was made when John Milner became vicar apostolic in 1803 and decided to live in Wolverhampton. While now the house at Oscott was not used for the purpose first intended, the accommodation it provided was otherwise useful. Towards the end of the eighteenth century Joseph Berrington, scholar and sometime chaplain to Sir John Throckmorton, came here to live. It was from Oscott, on 10 April 1787, that he issued a celebrated *Address to Protestant Dissenters*, in which he urged that both they and Catholics should – at a time when both were seeking independence – bury their prejudices. 'From the excesses of our progenitors', he wrote, 'we have both learned wisdom: let us then rejoice rather in our reformation, forget what is passed, and be friends'.[1]

There was also living at Oscott at that time Dr John Bew – an early student at Sedgeley who had enjoyed a distinguished academic career at Douai and latterly in Paris as superior of the Seminary of St Gregory's. Like many others he was obliged hurriedly to leave France. His arrival at Oscott was opportune.

To meet the need caused by the extinction of the familiar European seminaries, it was hoped that at Oscott, with the help of Bew, a small company of students could be educated for the Church. In 1794, however, on the initiative of certain influential Catholics of the region, a more ambitious scheme was projected. A prospectus, addressed 'to all classes of Catholics wishing for secondary education for their sons', indicated instruction being directed, on the one hand to religion and morals, and on the other, to classical studies and useful science. As a result of this initiative a college, with a handful of ecclesiastical students in residence, of which Bew was president, formally came into being in 1796. Three years later it was publicly advertised. By 1808 it was felt that there was need for more effective direction and organization, and for an administrator whose presence would be helpful in respect of fund-raising.

This brought John Milner, who was not only vicar apostolic of the district but a considerable influence on national events, into the organization as 'sole proprietor and director'. Rev Thomas Potts, a Douai priest who had acted as Bew's vice president, continued as administrator. In 1805 the new college was helped by a generous gift of £200 from John Rayment, of Britannia Square, Worcester.[2]

On 15 August 1808 a new constitution, originated by Milner – and to remain virtually unaltered for fifty years – was formally adopted for St Mary's College, Oscott. The formal opening of the college duly took place, but at that time there was little possibility of supporting it with more than the simplest musical offering:

> . . . the Litany of Loretto performed by the Jones family of Wolverhampton, accompanied by one of them on the pianoforte. The Litany was spun out and made the most of on the occasion, as little else was produced in the musical department.[3]

Later in the year attempts were made to establish a choir. One of the basses was Henry Weedall, whose father – a London doctor – was a friend of Bishop Milner. Having been first sent to the school at Sedgeley Park, near Wolverhampton (on Milner's advice), the young Weedall continued his studies at Oscott. In 1808 he wrote to his friend Arnold Knight:

> We have established a choir, very decent considering we are novices in improvements. It is intended after some time to get an organ and enlarge the chapel, but at present we are content with a harpsichord.[4]

Weedall stayed at Oscott to teach classics, and in 1814 was ordained priest by Milner. Although not trained as a musician, Weedall was an enthusiatic amateur. He was also a subscriber to Novello's *Music for the Portuguese Embassy Chapel*. Said to have had 'a clear flexible voice and a correct ear, he sang with great expression and precision'. Webbe's *Super flumina Babylonis* he interpreted with much feeling, while he covered a wide range of songs and glees. Of the latter he most esteemed Callcott's Ossian settings. As Professor of Theology and vice president of the College from 1818, Weedall exercized much influence in the early days of Oscott.

In 1826 he succeeded Bew as president. Before that time, however, he had enabled the college to make some progress on the musical front.

The prospectus of 1808 had left a little room for music, albeit if only as an 'extra' study: 'Approved masters of dancing, music and drawing, may be engaged, if required, from the neighbouring town of Birmingham'. In 1816 opportunity for the presentation of secular music was afforded by the building of a new Exhibition Room, which was used for this purpose in the following year. At the annual summer exhibition – the equivalent of speech day elsewhere – whatever instrumental music could be produced from the students' resources, and from zealous choristers who had glees and popular songs in their secular repertoire, was generally heard with approbation.

In the early years of the nineteenth century seminaries and colleges depended largely for music appropriate to ecclesiastical occasions on the simpler pieces from the familiar collections of Webbe and Novello. But with increasing skill and ambition popular movements from Masses by (or attributed to) Mozart and Haydn were undertaken. Before long the Catholic community at large became aware of the musical resources at the college, whose choristers were encouraged by invitations to perform on special occasions in the new churches being built throughout the Midlands. Such occasions also encouraged exploration of music of a more challenging character.

There was a close relationship between the college and neighbouring Birmingham. Here – as early as 1657 – the Franciscans had established a modest mission.[5] There was also a discreet Franciscan presence in a so-called 'mass-house' in the country, at Edgbaston. The first Catholic chapel in Birmingham was built in the last year of the reign of James II. After that it was not until 1786 that another chapel, dedicated to St Peter, was built. This too was served by Franciscans, the first priest in office being a Father Nutt. In 1807 a not very friendly notice in *The Gentleman's Magazine* indicated an intention to build a new chapel – to accommodate 'a great number of Catholics who attend to their duty, and also a great many others who have long neglected it'.[6] The new chapel, dedicated to St Chad, was opened in Shadwell Street in 1809. Here, from the beginning, music was regarded as a significant part of worship:

> .. the expanding spirit of the congregation sought far more than the mere necessaries of worship, and they desired to establish a choir, to add to the solemnity of religion. The services of Mr. Tebaye, a Catholic dancing-master, were engaged. He accompanied his wife with his violin. This was the first Catholic choir of Birmingham. Soon after Mr. [John] Hardman [I] presented the choir with an organ at a cost of £360.[7]

On 16 September 1821, to celebrate the opening of a new organ, special music was performed at both morning and evening services. The organist for the day was Thomas Munden, a well-known choral director and organist, closely associated with the Birmingham Festival. For the occasion he brought with him members of his own choral society. The order of Mass was detailed in the wordbook: Chorus, *Veni Creator Spiritus* (S Webbe); at the beginning of Mass – Chorus, *Kyrie* (V Novello) – Duet, *Christe* – Chorus, *Kyrie*; Before the Gospel – Chorus, *Gloria* (S Webbe jun); after the Sermon, *Benedicamus Domino* (Wesley), Chorus, *The Nicene Creed* (S Webbe jun); After the Creed – Solo, *In Te speravi* (S Webbe sen); Chorus, *Sanctus* (Novello); at the Elevation – Solo, *Panis angelicus* (Mozart); Semi-chorus, *Agnus Dei* (Natividad). In the evening there were items by Novello, Pergolesi, and David Perez.[8]

Two years later, on 24 August 1823, it being necessary to raise funds for the repair of the chapel, Special Sacred Music was again performed at morning and evening services. Movements from Masses by Mozart and Haydn, as well as from Haydn's *Creation*, were performed. An orchestra of strings with flute, oboe, two clarinets, two bassoons, two horns, two trumpets, two trombones, and timpani was led by Mr Shargool. W H Sharman – composer of a new setting of the *Tantum ergo* – was at the pianoforte. The preachers for the day, Dr Weedall and Rev John Abbot, were both from Oscott, with which the musical connection remained throughout the annual Special Services of 1825, 1826, and 1827. In 1827 selected movements from Handel's *Messiah* and *Israel in Egypt* – of which Latin translations of the words were available – were performed.

In 1827 Sharman, by now music director at Oscott, was well-known and active in a wider area;[9] while Charles Jeffries, an admired tenor soloist, as choirmaster, aroused enthusiasm for some of the repertory pieces of the glee clubs. The meaning of the term 'glee' was in this case somewhat extended. The most popular composer was Henry Bishop, but the elder Webbe's 'Glorious Apollo' found a regular place, while Callcott's Ossianic 'Peace to the Souls of the Heroes' was an essential item in an Exhibition programme. In the early years, there being students from Italy and Switzerland at the college, ethnic courtesy required occasional performance of appropriate Tyrolean and Italian pieces.

A general idea of choral music during his student days at Oscott was remembered by one distinguished alumnus, Bishop Francis Amherst:

> Our choir was not at all bad as choirs were in those days, very long before ecclesiastical music had received much attention. We thought Mozart's XII Mass the grandest effort of musical genius, and listened with delighted ears to Zingarelli's Laudate, which is no doubt very charming, but totally devoid of any ecclesiastical character.[10]

In 1836 the first stone of a new chapel at Oscott was laid as part of a programme of expansion. Recommended by his patron, the Earl of

Shrewsbury, Augustus Welby Northmore Pugin – 'not much more than two or three and twenty, beardless, with long, thick, straight black hair, an eye that took in everything, with genius and enthusiasm in every line of his features'[11] – was invited by Weedall to help in the project.

A year later he was appointed Professor of Ecclesiastical Architecture and Antiquities. Pugin's lectures were above the heads of his student audiences, but his recommendation of the combination of beauty and usefulness in stained glass gratified John Hardman II who, succeeding his father as head of the family business – Ecclesiastical Metal Works (founded 1830) – in close association with Pugin developed, as a separate company, the Stained Glass Works (1845). It was through Hardman's business sense, technical knowledge, and piety, that Pugin's ideas became nationally effective.[7]

In 1838 the opening of the new college building provided new opportunities for music. There was a new organ, the gift of John Hardman, and through the good offices of Nicholas Wiseman – rector of the English College in Rome – a German musician, Herr Johann Benz, was engaged as music director and lecturer in modern languages. Having studied in Rome with Giuseppe Baini – director of the Pontifical choir, and promoter of the Palestrinan tradition – he was eminently suitable to lead the students of Oscott into the brave new world of liturgical music as authenticated by contemporary scholarship.[12] Wiseman, however, despite his strong Roman connections, was personally in favour of 'modern music' rather than the approved Gregorian music of the Church.

An account of music at Oscott is recalled by James Plunket, a pupil of the school at the time:

> At Sedgley Park I had learned the piano and my uncle asked me if I would like to continue learning at Oscott. At the park my music had been carried on in playtime. At Oscott music was learned during school time. I am sorry to say that I grudged the time taken from my other studies, and declined my uncle's offer. My voice had broken, so that I was no longer in the choir, and my musical experiences were suspended. Still I had the advantage of hearing the grand church services given in splendid style under the direction of a German musician who was also the organist. Specially noteworthy were the Lamentations as sung in the Sistine Chapel at Rome. These were sung by eight voices, none of them in unison, and the singers were grouped round the German maestro in the choir, not the gallery. He had his violin and used it to keep up any voice which his acute ear detected in fluttering.[13]

St Chad's Cathedral, Birmingham

In January 1834 at a meeting presided over by Milner's successor, Bishop Thomas Walsh, a resolution, moved by Rev T McDonnell, priest at St

Peter's Chapel, called for support for the erection of 'a commodious and splendid Catholic Church worthy of the metropolis of the Midland District'. The project moved slowly, but with the injection of part of the considerable private inheritance of Bishop Walsh, with the hope of public funds being available after Birmingham received its charter of incorporation in 1838, and with the acceptance of a design by Pugin, it was announced early in the new year that work should commence on the new church under the architect's direction. On 9 November the *Orthodox Journal* reported 'The Ceremony of Blessing and laying the Foundation Stone at St Chad's Church, Birmingham'.

By now Nicholas Wiseman was both president of Oscott and coadjutor bishop. Pugin and his inseparable ally Phillipps were discovering that Wiseman's opinions on the relationship of the arts to religion were not ones which they shared. By education, through his long years of service on a high level at the centre of the Church, and by natural inclination, Wiseman was not persuaded that Gothic style was necessarily the most suitable for churches. Nor did he undervalue the spiritual qualities of the music of Mozart and Haydn. Musically he had been well educated, played the piano and the organ, and for some time had acted as organist of the English College in Rome. Propaganda[14] was not well disposed to approve aesthetic eccentricity in England and forbade mediaeval-style liturgical inventiveness. So far as Wiseman was concerned, however much Pugin was patronized by aesthetic aristocrats, he was 'an architect recently converted from heresy'.

At the end of 1840 Pugin was greatly disturbed, for a major part of his design for the church (as for all churches, if possible) was a rood-screen – a subject immediately ripe for discord. The rood-screen was designed so as 'to afford a tolerable idea of the sublime effect of the ancient rood-screens before their mutilation under Edward the Sixth', and also 'to mark the separation between the faithful and the sacrifice, the nave and the church'.[15] Although musical arrangements were outside his competence, with the dedication of the new church in view, he nevertheless wrote to Phillipps:

> As you say, till the old Gregorian Music is restored, nothing can be done, but of how I almost despair – I do indeed, I built a solemn church at Southport. It was to be opened with a perfectly disgusting display and a bill ending with an Ordinary at 2 o'clock, 3/6 each.[16]

St Chad's Church was solemnly dedicated on 23 January 1841 in the presence of nine vicars apostolic, thirteen bishops and 150 priests. The choir of Oscott College was present under the direction of Johann Benz, who by now had resigned his appointment at Oscott to undertake direction of the music of the new church. The music at the Dedication consisted

principally of an unpublished Mass by Haydn. Walsh presided over the
Pontifical High Mass and the sermon was preached by Wiseman. Among
others, Weedall also took part in the ceremony.

In his sermon Wiseman spoke eloquently of the changing nature of
public worship, alluding within it to the function of art.

> The interior of our chapels, bare and unembellished, contained no more
> than sufficed for the performance of our religious acts; their exterior was
> hardly marked by any distinguishable symbol of Catholic belief; — the very
> cross seemed but timidly placed upon their summits. Gradually, efforts have
> been made to pass from this stage of abasement to one worthier of our
> religion and of our condition; our churches have assumed a form which at
> once fits them for their purpose, and precludes their being mistaken for places
> destined to any other worship. Their proportions have been enlarged, their
> sanctuaries ennobled, and every essential part more carefully provided. And
> in addition to this, more attention has been paid to such ornament as
> becomes the beauty of God's spouse.[17]

In the new church, of which Benz was organist for the first three years
after its dedication, John Hardman acted as choirmaster. The character of
the music undertaken is indicated by the entries in the Registers of music
from 2 July 1843 to 3 March 1844:

Sunday	2 July:	Mass — Drobisch
	9 July:	Kyrie, Gloria, Sanctus, Agnus Dei — Haydn No 7
		Offertory — Drobisch
Thursday	13 July:	Solemn High Mass & Dirge; Rt Rev Peter Augustine Baines, VA Western District — Gregorian Mass
Sunday	16 July:	Kyrie — Mozart No 1, Gloria, Sanctus, Agnus Dei — Mozart No 7
		Offertory: Ave Maria — Drobisch
Wednesday	19 July:	Opening of Church of St Benedict, Kemerton: Pontifical High Mass, with Choir from Birmingham — Misses Souter, Betts, Early, Davis, Powell, Smith, Powell, Jones, Johnston, Mark Carith and Thomas Bishop
		Kyrie, Gloria, Credo, Sanctus (Agnus Dei) Haydn No 13
Sunday	23 July:	Kyrie, Gloria, Sanctus — Mozart No 3
		Agnus Dei — Caldara
	30 July:	Preacher Bishop Walsh; Kyrie — Mozart No 1
		Gloria — Diabelli, Credo — Drobisch
		Offertory, Qui confidunt — Ernesto Eberlin

		Departure of Mr. Benz, Organist of St. Chad's, Birmingham
	6 August:	Kyrie, Gloria, Sanctus – Haydn No 13 Offertory, Adoro Te, Agnus dei – [Stephen] Paxton
		Organ by young Bitton of Oscot [sic]
	13 August:	Agnus Dei – Webbe in F minor
		New Organist arrived Mr. Leipold
	20 August:	Mozart No 7
	9 October:	Benigne fac
	15 October:	Gregorian Mass, M Leipold having hurt his finger
	22 October:	Kyrie, Gloria – Mozart No 3, Offertory – harmonized Gregorian, for Trinity Sunday, Sanctus – Mozart No 3, Agnus Dei – Haydn No 7
	29 October:	[Rev J Moore?] Absent in London at [Our Lady of the Assumption and St Gregory] Warwick Street; Preacher [at St Chad's] John Maguire D D
	26 November:	Rinck, Miserere – M Haydn
	3 December:	Kyrie, Sanctus, Agnus Dei – Harmonized Gregorian, Palestrina
	17 December:	Offertory : Rorate, Palestrina from Motetts
Sunday	25 December:	3rd Mass, Offertory: Hodie – Benz

1844

	25 February:	Gregorian Mass in small gallery

In 1846 Alfred Novello issued a volume entitled *Cantica Sacra or Gregorian Music consisting of / Masses Graduals/Offertories/Hymns and Motets . . . for the use of/Catholic Choirs/with Full Organ Accompaniments* by J B Benz Esq, lately director of music at St Mary's College and at St Chad's Birmingham. Benz contributed a Preface, to be praised for its realistic view of the general situation.

He understood how difficult it was for most chapels to establish choirs. Even when there was a choir it was difficult to find copies of suitable music. The temptation to try to perform elaborate music – particularly the Masses of Mozart and Haydn – was to be resisted.Too often such attempts ended in failure. But two or three voices 'of ordinary tone and power', supported by a simple organ accompaniment, could very well effectively perform the simple chants of the church. Benz concluded his exhortation by defining the minimum requirements of an organist:

> . . . If there be but one person in the congregation who can play the organ, so far as to make simple chords, without great power of execution, it is enough to secure the pleasing and edifying accession of sacred music to the Church offices. He may select three or four persons of ordinary intelligence, and with fair sonorous voices, and in a few weeks instruct them sufficiently to be able to execute the music of the present work.

Benz, who left Birmingham to be organist of St Anne's Cathedral in Leeds, is remembered in St Chad's by a figure representing St Cecilia, in the north aisle of the newly designated cathedral, given by him in 1850. In this same year John Hardman made an endowment of £50 annually for the newly designated cathedral, on condition that,

> the Kyrie, Gloria, and Agnus Dei, except during the seasons of Lent and Advent, and the Sundays before mentioned, may, at the discretion of the choirmaster, be sung in harmonised music in the spirit and ecclesiastical style of Palestrina, or the purely vocal school of the grave and severer kind, which admits of the accompaniment of the organ only, but nevertheless requires no such accompaniment, and is complete without it.[18]

In 1848 William Bernard Ullathorne became vicar apostolic of the Midland District, in succession to Thomas Walsh, and was installed in St Chad's Cathedral. Two years later, on the establishment of the episcopacy, he became the first Bishop of Birmingham. A remarkable man in every way, Ullathorne was deeply affected by music.[19] Early in his episcopate, on 8 March 1855, Ullathorne wrote to Phillipps de Lisle:

> You will be glad to hear that congregational singing is among the most marked signs of progress which I find in the diocese. Plain chant at Benediction is another of the improvements which is spreading, and generally, a graver order of music . . . .
> I hope in a few weeks to send you a pastoral on plain chant from my pen, with annotations. I lectured on the subject last Sunday at Oscott. The more I study the subject the more surprise I feel that it has been so much neglected and so little understood.[20]

As if in response to this on 14 September 1856 John Hardman ii, who had taken over his father's role as benefactor to the cathedral, proposed further endowment of the choir in the interest from £1000, 'on the condition of singing strictly Ecclesiastic Music'.

Ullathorne was insistent that the music performed throughout his diocese should be of a high order of decency. His principles were those which were later to be found in the *Motu proprio* of Pius x in 1903. The cathedral, he believed, should be a school to the diocese of what is best, according to the spirit and laws of the church, in parochial administration, in rubrical law, and in ecclesiastical song. And such, I believe, it is generally recognised to be throughout the diocese.[21]

In 1880 he published CHURCH MUSIC: *A Discourse, Given in St. Chad's Cathedral, on the half Jubilee of its Choir.* A general survey of Catholic Church music, with injunctions concerning performance and interpretation. which accords with the then most recent official view of the church, expressed in an Encyclical of Benedict XIV, published in 1750.

As a comprehensive account of the history of music in the church, insofar as this was possible to contain within small space, it stands out both by its pastoral concern and by its musical insights. The conclusion is typically broad in concept:

> Handel was conducting his choir through an oratorio. In an address to the Almighty their voices rose loud and streperous in the ostentation of their art. The great composer, with hand, low voice, and a look of awe, broke in upon them: 'Hush!' he said. 'In the presence of the great God would you shout and scream?' The whole spirit of the music of the Mass is in these words.

Old habits died hard. On 26 November 1881 the Bishop, having read an article in a Birmingham journal[22] about a recent performance of Mozart's Twelfth Mass – with orchestra – in the Church of St Mary and St John, Wolverhampton, wrote to the parish priest, Canon Davies:

> You will see the use made of your name in the enclosed article headed 'What we hear'. There have been such excesses at St Michael's Birmingham, making the mass an exhibition instead of a devotion as far as the music is concerned, that I have been obliged to prohibit the abuse. After reading the enclosed, will you kindly tell me the facts.

Ullathorne retired from his bishopric in 1888 (he died in the next year) and was succeeded by Edward Ilsley, who had worked closely with him for some years. Ilsley, a former student of Oscott, had been appointed by Ullathorne as rector of a newly established Diocesan Seminary established in Olton, in Staffordshire, in 1873 and six years later he became auxiliary Bishop. Throughout his life Ilsley was a keen musician, playing the organ and often taking singing practices. For thirty years he was parish priest in Longton, the southernmost town of the Potteries, where he established the Church of St Gregory and the adjacent school. Like Newman he was always ready to teach music to the children of his school, and to maintain choral music in the town. In his later days, as Bishop, Ilsley took great pains in the proper presentation of the cathedral music.[23] In 1904 Pope Pius X sent congratulations to Bishop Ilsley 'on the good example set by the Cathedral Choir in the rendering of Gregorian chant'.[24]

Notes

1 Sir John Throckmorton was a member of a Catholic Committee established in 1779 (reformed in 1787) to enlist political support for further measures to relieve discrimination. Berrington's principal works: *State and Behaviour of English Catholics from the Revolution to the Year 1780, An Address to Protestant Dissenters*, Oscott, 10 April, 1787.

2 See Chapter 3, p 39.

3 Church of St Peter and St Paul, Wolverhampton, see Husenbeth, *The Life of the Right Reverend Monsignor Weedall D D*, London, 1860, p 34.

4 Husenbeth, p 5.

5 Register of 1657, Birmingham Archdiocesan Archives.
  In 1688 a Franciscan, Leo Randolph, built a chapel in Birmingham, which did not long survive. A hundred years later, Father Nutt, also a Franciscan, built the chapel of St Peter, which lasted until 1969.

6 *GM*, 1807, vol II, p 197.

7 Creaney: *Saint Chad's Cathedral*, p 19. John Hardman (1767–1844), of a Lancashire recusant family, established a business, in the first instance, for button and medal manufacture in Birmingham, which was taken over by his son John.

8 Wordbooks in Birmingham Public Library (Local History).

9 Leicester, *Catholic Worcester*, p 35.

10 Roskell, *Memoirs of F.K.Amherst*, London, 1903, p 129.

11 Ibid, pp 13–14.

12 Guiseppe Baini (1775–1844), maestro di cappella Papal choir, author of *Life of Palestrina*, 1828.

13 James Plunket, *Autobiography* (MS), p 62, Library of Oscott College.

14 Propaganda, the Congregation at the Vatican responsible for Catholic missions in countries without an established Catholic hierarchy.

15 Pugin, *Ecclesiastical Architecture*, pp 78–79; cf Phillipps II 125; the rood-screen was in due course removed from St Chad's to Holy Trinity, Reading.

16 Phillipps II, 213.

17 Nicholas Wiseman, *A Sermon preached at the Dedication of St Chad's Cathedral, Birmingham*, London/Birmingham, 1841, p 10.

18 Creaney, op cit p 19. John Hardman, persuaded by Pugin of the importance of Gregorian chant, was assisted in determining the character of the music in St Chad's Cathedral by John Lambert of Salisbury (see Chapter 5, n 17). A great benefactor to many Catholic causes in Birmingham, he was (as well as controlling the interests of his firm) choirmaster in the Cathedral for eighteen years.

19 *Autobiography of Archbishop Ullathorne, with Selections from Letters*, p 20.

20 *Letters of Archbishop Ullathorne*, pp 66–7.

21 Ibid, p 401.

22 *The Dart, A Journal of Sense and Satire*, Birmingham, 25 November 1881.

23 Chadwick, Owen, *The Victorian Church*, II, 1970, p 410.

24 In 1897 St Mary's College, Oscott was created a Central Seminary and, under the Rector, Dr Parkinson, the old Ratisbon and Mechlin books were discarded in favour of the principles established by Dom Pothier at Solesmes. Richard Runciman Terry, organist at Downside was a frequent visitor to Oscott for the revived St Cecilia's Day festivals.

5 Stylistic Authority

In the last years of the eighteenth century a new generation of ecclesiastical architects had sought to serve the requirements of the principal religious denominations with what were suggested as appropriate architectural styles. For a time the Church of England encouraged Greek Classical – mostly in London – and early neo-Gothic – mostly in the country. On the general principle of avoiding a style historically associated with the established church, Catholics often tended to prefer a classical plan. But the advocacy of architects who combined technical ability with an appreciation of history made the case for Gothic almost irresistible to those searching for the ancient practices and habiliments of Christianity.

The careful publications of John Britton (1771–1857), including *Architectural Antiquities of Great Britain*, with views, plans, elevations, and sections, in four volumes, between 1805 and 1814, to be followed by a supplementary volume, and *A Chronological History and Graphic Illustrations of Christian Architecture in Great Britain* [1818–1826] were encouraging reading for practical men. In 1819, Thomas Rickman, a Birmingham architect, in *An Attempt to Discriminate the Styles of English Architecture from the Conquest to the Reformation,* noted how

> During the eighteenth century, various attempts, under the name of Gothic, have arisen in repairs and rebuilding ecclesiastical edifices, but these have been little more than making clustered columns and pointed windows, every real principle of English architecture being, by the builders, either unknown or totally neglected.[1]

For the first time, the definitions of English architecture which have remained in general use were then stated:

English architecture, may be divided into four distinct periods or styles, which may be named.

1st: the Norman style
2nd: the Early English style
3rd: the decorated English style, and
4th: the Perpendicular English style.

In 1791 a Catholic Relief Act was passed which permitted a Catholic chapel to be built, provided there was neither tower or bell. John Milner, at the time pastor of the Catholic congregation in Winchester, was a keen and informed student of architecture.[2] With characteristic determination, after the passage of the Act of 1791, in the next year, taking advantage of the authority afforded by the recent Act, he had a chapel built to his design for his congregation.

This, in Gothic style, was the first Catholic church to have been built in England since the Reformation. In *A Treatise on the Ecclesiastical Architecture of England, During the Middle Ages* (1811) he gave this robust support to his preference for Gothic:

> But why should we wander into every remote country in the known world, and into the region of fancy, in search of an invention which belongs to our own climate? And for what purpose should we take so much pains to prove a plant to be an imported exotic which we actually see sprouting up and attaining its full growth in our own garden?[3]

— a naturalistic sentiment similarly expressed in respect of English music a century later by Ralph Vaughan Williams:

> English music is like the tree which flowers once in a hundred years: but unless the tree were alive there would be no flower and its life depends, not only on its own intrinsic vitality but on the soil on which it grows, the rain that falls on it and the sun which shines on it . . .[4]

By 1798 Augustus Charles Pugin (1762–1832) — a refugee from the consequences of the French Revolution — had just arrived in England, and had begun work as a draughtsman in the office of John Nash. It was his task to make coloured views of the mansions on which Nash at any time happened to be working. Pugin himself quickly gained a reputation as a reliable exponent of various branches of technology, craft and design. He reached a wider, appreciative public by the excellence of his drawings of English Gothic buildings. In these the exact proportions of arches and decorative features were perfectly conveyed, and the improprieties of what was passing as Gothic were noticed from his *Specimens of Gothic Architecture* (1821–1823).

Much of the cultural history of England during the nineteenth century was associated with Pugin's son, Augustus Welby Pugin (1812–1852) who, in a singular manner, managed to address all the aesthetic and ritualistic problems of a reviving Catholic tradition at the same time. Educated at Christ's Hospital, where John Shaw's Hall, of 1820 Gothic revival, was set against the remains of the ancient Greyfriars cloisters, Pugin early felt the critical urge. The newer buildings of the school, he later complained, 'although they certainly are free from the absurdities of paganism', were 'strange piles of debased design'.[5]

Leaving school, Pugin was apprenticed to his father. Inheriting his father's skills in drawing, and his wider interests, he first applied himself to design in general. His independence began to establish itself when – on account of a commission passed on by his father – he designed the furniture for Wyattville's Romantic reworking of Windsor Castle. A theatrical strain in his nature was encouraged by exercises in designing stage machinery and painting scenery. In 1831 he was made responsible for the scenery for one of a number of plays, melodramas and ballets based on Scott's novel *Kenilworth*.

A year later Pugin's life was redirected when the sixteenth Earl of Shrewsbury, impressed by his talents in the design of furniture, engaged him to assist in the refurnishing of Alton Towers, his mansion in Staffordshire. In its Romantic setting this great house became a launching site for the total reclamation of the Gothic character – in thought, word and deed. Shrewsbury's piety, wealth and influence were funnelled through Pugin into the building of churches, schools, colleges and seminaries, first across the Midlands, and then across England and Ireland.

The subsequent history of the revival of English Gothic in all its ramifications, as well as in its exported versions to English-speaking countries, is as remarkable as it seemed logical to George Gilbert Scott:

> I am convinced that the revived love for our old buildings, followed as it was subsequently by a desire to imitate their architecture, was as spontaneous and as irresistible a movement of the human mind as those which had originated either Classic or mediaeval art, or that which, two thousand years after its first rise, had led to the revival of the former.[6]

Pugin and Shrewsbury were joined in the realization of their ideals by Ambrose de Lisle Phillipps, owner of a newly built Tudor mansion in Grace Dieu, Leicestershire. Like Shrewsbury, Phillipps was a convert to Roman Catholicism, ardent to represent the faith in new, worthy and meaningful architecture, and – insofar as his published essays were concerned – a personal form of antiquated English. The significant monument to Phillipps's sense of purpose was the Cistercian church and monastery of Mount St Bernard's. Set in a strikingly picturesque situation, enhanced by the Calvary and Stations of the Cross not otherwise to be seen in post-Reformation England, this new foundation attracted many notable visitors.

The combination of Shrewsbury, Phillipps and Pugin released a flood of patronage, raised to the level of pious devotion, without parallel since the Middle Ages. Music was anciently acknowledged to claim a special place of honour in religious observance and both Pugin and Phillipps, without modesty, frequently expressed their opinions on this subject.

Phillipps wrote an ambitious lecture, 'On Church Musick and the Ecclesiastical Chaunt' which was addressed to 'the Choir of Grace Dieu and Whitwick'. In this essay, of which only part survived, the principal interest concerns Phillipps's own early experiences and ambitions. Like Pugin he was particularly susceptible to music enhanced by an appropriate physical setting. So he told how, during the autumn of 1828, when in the Basilica of St Sabina in Rome, he experienced an unforgettable 'sublime moment' when 'the monks to whom it belongs were just chanting the concluding antiphons of the compline hour'.[7] Then it was that he realised that:

> At the present day in our English Catholick Chapels and Churches the antient Church musick has been almost totally abandoned, and instead of it has been substituted a light and indecorous style of singing far more calculated to express the feeling of earthly passion than the grace and solemn effects of true Christian devotion.[8]

Pugin's sensitivities were exposed to more violent effects. He recalled how once when he was in Cologne cathedral

> An orchestral crash commenced what must have been intended for the 'Kyrie'. The mighty pillars, arches, vaults, all seemed to disappear; I was no longer in a cathedral, but at a Concert Musard or a Jardine.[9]

Once fired with a determination to purify the arts, Pugin reified the indecorous. Having been employed in the theatre at the beginning of his career, he waxed eloquent over the theatricality associated with the opening of new churches:

> Bills of the performance are circulated, worded and lettered in the manner which a musical director with a travelling company would put forth on arriving in a country town. On one occasion Madame Stockhausen, the Star of the day, headed the list, then the names of some second rates and of the conductor or leader succeeded in due order. Even the clergy were played in like soldiers to parade. Procession march! occasional overture! – so said the bills – choruses, duets, quartets, fuges [*sic*], sermon, collection, solos etc, succeeded in rapid succession; and what began with an overture, ended in true theatrical style; with a finale.[10]

He took particular exception to a new church in classical style in Hereford. Dedicated to St Francis Xavier, it stood in Broad Street, across from and challenging the cathedral. Pugin disapproved of the building at once. Many such churches – resembling, on the one hand, a dancing-room and, on the other, a mechanics' institute – were being erected, he suggested. Their purpose was to provide easy entertainment in the music rather than the traditional chants of the church. This new church at Hereford might be fitly termed the new Catholic Concert Room, he said. In fact, for the opening of the church the best Catholic music available in the region was performed.[11]

In a final fusillade aimed at musical impropriety Pugin protested

> What shall the Song of Simeon, the Hymn of St. Ambrose, the Canticles of
> our Blessed Lady herself, give place to modern effusions? Shall we tolerate
> the conversion of the liturgy into a song-book?[12]

In 1837 the young Pugin put before the public a book, of which the
purpose was to turn the nation away from the aesthetic follies of modern
times and to retreat into the felicities of the Middle Ages. *Contrasts; or, A
Parallel between the Architecture of the 15th and 19th Centuries*, was
published in Salisbury (where Pugin was then living) in 1836.

In this vituperative work, described by George Gilbert Scott as 'an
architectural *jeu d'esprit*',[13] Pugin notified his repudiation of the Church of
England. He also effectively soured the climate of debate in respect of
architecture by showing examples of the worst of the modern and the best
of the ancient. The beautiful precision of his drawings merely aggravated
the unfairness of the argument. The Catholic church, he maintained, was
the sole repository of Christian Art. At that time Pugin, with some justice,
might well have thought that was true.

A general lack of interest in church art and architecture shown by the
Established Church at the time was paralleled by a general indifference on
the part of the laity to any issues of theological concern. Pugin further
aggravated the situation in *An Apology for a Work entitled 'Contrasts'*,
which was published in Birmingham.

Here he stated what had previously been suggested, but with a greater
enthusiasm. Because of a lack of Catholic feeling among its 'professors',
and an absence of ecclesiastical patronage, and the 'apathy with which a
Protestant nation must necessarily treat the higher branches of Art', the
Arts were 'degraded'.[14] In the cathedrals of the Established Church a 'daily
mockery of worship was enacted', by 'worldly men . . . resolved to worship
God by proxy', who had

> accordingly . . . abandoned the Choir to the chorister-boys and singing-men,
> – a set of wretched hirelings, whose salaries are so small, that they are obliged to
> follow trades and secular employments, in order to gain a livelihood.[15]

As for the laity, all that interested most of them was the singing. They
took no part in the service, but waited until the anthem was announced. As
soon as that was finished, they hurried out.

There was substance in what Pugin was saying (it had been said more
than once in the eighteenth century) and there were those in the Church of
England who agreed with him. John Jebb, Frederick Gore Ouseley, and
Thomas Helmore were already attending to the elimination of improprieties,
the reclamation of Gregorian chant, and the preservation of liturgical decency
in cathedral worship.[16]

As for Phillipps, much of his leisure was dedicated to the preparation of material with which a knowledge of, and competence in sacred music might be fostered. Carried away by fervour, he quite disregarded practicality. For example, some of his 'plain-chaunt' manuals were so beautifully, and Gothicly, printed, that they were rendered unreadable. *A Little Gradual or Chorister's Companion*, supported by prayers from Breviary or Missal, prepared for the benefit of his own establishment choristers, being confined in double columns became invisible. As well as the prominent place he occupied in the movement for the renewal of Catholicism, the conduct of worship in Phillipps's chapel from time to time brought important visitors to Grace Dieu. Among them was John Lambert, a Catholic lawyer in Salisbury with a distinguished record in public affairs, who not only protected the citizenly rights of Catholics but was also concerned that they should have access to their musical heritage.[17] Equally diligent in publication as Phillipps, Lambert was more practical. In 1848 he published *The true mode of accompanying the Gregorian Chant*; in 1854, *Music of the Middle Ages, especially in relation to its Rhythm and Mode of Execution*. He published a *Vesper Psalter* in 1850, *Catholic Sacred Songs* in 1853, and collections for children. His services to church music were recognized by his membership of the Academy of St Cecilia in Rome, and the award of a gold medal by Pope Pius IX.

The revival of 'English Church Architecture' successfully moved through the nineteenth century on the Gothic impulse provided by Pugin and continued, and varied, by his son Edward Welby Pugin, Gilbert Scott and – among others – George Edmund Street, John Pollard Seddon and his partner John Pritchard, all aware of the imperious presence of John Ruskin.[18] Where opinions were expressed, or dogmas issued, in respect of music appropriate to the Gothic climate, where Pugin was it was inevitable that Gregorian chant should be proposed. But in comparison with the state of architecture Gregorian chant ran an uncertain course. Both clergy and laity continued to need persuasion of its missionary merits. A good deal of piety was confused with muddled thinking.

In 1818 a fairly muted suggestion had been made by Charles Butler, that there should be some attempt to restore the Gregorian song to the English Catholic chapels. In respect of performing style, the author suggested that

> ... if the antient Gregorian Masses were sung, as they might be sung, with a little more care and practice, would not more pleasure be given to a great majority of hearers, and more devotion excited in all? The solo verses should be sung by the general body of the congregation, in exact measure, and with subdued voices. The accompaniment on the organ, should be that, which we hear from our incomparable musical friend, Mr. Novello; chaste not meagre, learned not crude, full, not overpowering. A service thus performed, would delight, would instruct, would proselitize.[19]

The relationship between architecture and music was intensified in a period in which historic, philosophical, theological and musical consider-ations came together in a search for doctrinal probity. This was the inspiration both of Catholic and Evangelical musical activity in the period of Victorian reform. In a general way Newman's friend and pupil, Isaac Williams,[20] extended Pugin's elevation of the Gothic into his remarkable, detailed, versification of architectural design of *The Cathedral: or the Catholic and Apostolic Church in England*, published soon after the issue of Pugin's *Contrasts*.

The Romantic tendency inspires in Williams a sense of the appropriate-ness of particular music to particular areas of 'The Cathedral'. For 'The Choir' the extensive 'Sacramental Hymn', assigned to Men and to Angels, anticipates the imagery of Newman's angelic hymn. But there is also 'Village Psalmody' with the play of 'a gleam of song', united with the grander sounds of the cathedral – 'tis no wold fire, / But sparks, tho' scatter'd, from a heaven-strung lyre. / Thus, when the cloud of music roll'd along / Fills the melodious dome, blest sounds inspire / Each cloistral nook, vocal with sacred song.' Within the lyrical concept there is a sense of liturgical discipline , contrasting with the indulgence of William Sotheby's *Netley Abbey*.[21]

A fresh consideration of the relationship between words and music was required at a time when an enquiring respect for 'ancient' music, was marked by Stafford Smith's *Musica Antiqua* (1812) – 'A Selection of Music ... from the commencement of the twelfth to the beginning of the eighteenth century'. This significant work marked the first stage in the serious, scientific, study of music in England. The pull of history – whether in the Roman or the Anglican Church – put a special premium on Gregorian chant, for practical purposes a mode of expression in which authenticity in delivery hung on a slender Benedictine thread. The Congregation of Solesmes was founded – with the intention of scholarly research into, and exactness in the performance of, plainsong – in 1833.

An increasing diversification of tone colour in every area of music in the nineteenth century had a profound effect on emotional responses to sacred music in general. Within the ambit of Pugin's principles and skills music increasingly moved away from liturgical control – in spite of attempts to realize a liturgical purity of intention – and into its own idealized realm. The works which in Catholic church music propagated musical values were the Masses of Mozart and Haydn and other music generally, inspired by continental examples. For practical purposes what was considered ideal continued to lose out in the battle to strengthen the faith in fresh territories. As well as satisfying the faithful, the possibility of drawing Protestants towards the 'old faith' was never entirely out of the missionary mind. On these occasions there was often displayed a notable degree of neighbourly warmth, as Methodist and Church of England neighbours contributed musical skills to a common end. Music, with its own mystical authority, was irresistible.

The consecration of a new Catholic church was an opportunity for display. The streets of many dark urban centres were illuminated on these occasions by the brightness of vestments (never seen before) and by echoes of antiquity in unfamiliar, sacred music: Gregorian chant. The confidence with which Catholics faced the future after 1829 is illustrated by the establishment of new churches in the great industrial centres of Lancashire and Yorkshire, where there was also an established enthusiasm for music.

At a time when the search for an acceptable architectural style was hardly yet ended, it was of interest that the new St Patrick's chapel in Manchester – opened in March 1832 – was 'a very neat edifice in the Grecian style',[22] while the Catholic chapel which opened in Huddersfield six months later was 'a very beautiful Gothic edifice'.[23] So far as music was concerned there was a degree of agreement in presenting Mozart's Twelfth Mass – 'one of the first compositions of that great master, abounding in that solemnity, gravity, tenderness, and devotion, which breathes in his sacred compositions'.

On 8 May Pugin's second wife, Louisa Burton, whom he had married in 1833, was received into the church. The ceremony took place in a setting of impeccable Romantic charm, in St Peter's Chapel in the Earl of Shrewsbury's Alton Towers. At high mass, the 'Veni Creator Spiritus', in the 'old Salisbury Chaunt which the choir continued with impressive effect', captured the attention of 'the crowd which filled the chapel [and which] consisted chiefly of protestants, who beheld the ceremony with the most respectful and praiseworthy attention'.[24]

On 10 July of the same year, a new church at Everingham, in the East Riding of Yorkshire, was opened with a Pontifical high mass. This was a grand affair. Rev Dr Newsham of Ushaw College was at the organ and the choir 'embraced singers from the Cathedral, Catholic Chapel, and Choral Society of this city [York].[25] The music consisted of Haydn's Mass No 1, *Alma Virgo*, and Hummel, *Te Deum*.

In anticipation of the fifth anniversary of the opening of the Catholic church in Huddersfield, on 26 September, 1839, at which Nicholas Wiseman, rector of the English College in Rome, was to preach, the preliminary notices announced 'A most splendid selection of sacred music, with the performance by an efficient Choir'. The composers represented were Haydn, Mozart, Zingarelli and Romberg, and the 'most eminent Vocal Performers were engaged for the day'.[26]

For Nicholas Wiseman this was an opportunity to discover how distant from the Roman ideal was the music performed in English Catholic churches. Less than a year later, Wiseman, having been consecrated Bishop, was sent back to England by Pope Gregory XVI, as president of Oscott College. Soon after his return to England Pugin drew the attention of Phillipps to the opening of a church in Keighley, in Yorkshire, on 18 December 1840. There was, he reported,

> ... a most horrible scene. Not only was all decorum violated, but a regular row took place between the musicians, who quarrelled about their parts in the church, and after one hour's delay one priest drew off the singers and a Miss Whitwell – whose name appeared in the bills in gigantic letters – quavered away in most extraordinary style ....
>
> I quite agree with you that we shall do nothing without the real church music and where are we to find it? At your private chapel, where it is heard under every disadvantage for want of a good sounding church, powerful music, powerful choir organ etc.[27]

The manner in which congregations were being directed further and further away from the primary purpose of church music – according to Catholic tradition and discipline – is illustrated by the kind of services which took place on 1 June 1841, in St Augustine's Church, Preston, on the occasion of the installation of a new organ. Built by Robert Gray, one of a celebrated and well-established family firm, and exhibited by him, the virtues of the organ were thus presented:

> Of the different stops – each so perfect in its character, – it would be difficult to select the best; but if we might give an opinion as to which appeared to us the most unique [!], we should say the magnificent 'hautboy', in the swell, exceeds, in delicacy and fulness of tone, any we have previously heard. The pedal notes are exceedingly fine, even in power, and remarkably prompt to the touch of the performer; of ample volume to support the most elaborate structure of harmony which may be raised above them, yet so round and mellow as to form a beautiful accompaniment to the soft notes of the swell and choir organ.[28]

For the morning service movements were taken from Haydn's third and sixth Masses, and the Sanctus from Mozart's Requiem. In the evening the music included choruses by Handel and Haydn.

In the same year Pugin's *True Principles of Pointed or Christian Architecture* was published. George Gilbert Scott generously described this work as

> ... a gigantic step in advance. It grappled at once with all the fallacies which had corrupted modern architecture, and established a code of rules, founded upon common sense, utility and truth; while his *Apology* which came out a little later, showed the necessity of falling back upon our national style, and its ready applicability to every requirement of our day ... Not only were the advances he made in the revival of Pointed architecture most rapid, showing genius in every touch, – this was, in fact, the smallest of his achievements, –

he actually revived by his own personal exertions nearly every one of its subsidiary arts, architectural carving and sculpture, stained glass, decorative painting, metal work, enamelling, embroidery, woven textures, paper hangings, encaustic tiles, the manufacture of furniture, and even of ordinary household crockery ware, – all felt the impress of his hand and of his genius.[29]

But Scott omitted music.

Pugin's last shots in the battle to preserve the heritage of sacred music – delivered in 1850 through *An Earnest Appeal for the Revival of the Ancient Plain Song* – were singularly well aimed. Some of the targets still stand.

> It is, indeed, seriously proposed to change the whole nature of the divine services of the Catholic Church, under the specious pretext of rendering them more popular and adapting them to the spirit of the age.
> ... this monstrous proposal will be the means of awakening the ecclesiastical authorities to the necessity of restoring the ancient chant in all its purity ... the hired musicians (frequently heretics and infidels) who perform in a gallery ... [ensure that] the congregation is reduced to the position of listeners.

In Europe it was even worse. Taking note of the concert-like character of music in the Flemish cathedrals, Pugin turned to the recent desecration of the Basilica of St Francis, in Assisi, by the Franciscans themselves.

> ... the church was inundated with fiddles from all parts of the neighbouring country, and this most glorious church converted into a perfect *salle d'opera.*[30]

Pugin did not live long enough to become a great Victorian, but he was one of the dominating influences of the nineteenth century. Although the Christianity of the Middle Ages, of which his expression remains in countless churches and cathedrals, was his inspiration, he was relentlessly practical. A uniquely gifted craftsman, he gave opportunity through his designs in wood, metal and glass, to others to fashion objects that were both beautiful and useful. Pugin's relationship to music was of a different order. He was moved by the idea of music rather than by music itself. But his critical observations on the practice of music in worship were timely.

Notes

1 Thomas Rickman, *English Architecture*, 1819, pp 13–14.
2 John Milner, educated Sedgeley Park School and Douai; 1771 priest at Winchester; 1803 Bishop, vicar apostolic Midland District and active in reestablishment of St Mary's College, Oscott; a powerful influence in the movement for Emancipation; Fellow of the Society of Antiquaries.
3 Milner, *A Treatise on Ecclesiastical Architecture* etc, London, J Taylor, 1811, ded Duke of Norfolk, p 77.

4 Hadow, W H, *English Music*, 1931, Introduction, p ix.
5 Ferrey, *Recollections*, p 33.
6 Scott, G G, *Lectures on the Rise and Development of Mediaeval Architecture*, 1879, pp 316–17.
7 Purcell, *Phillips de Lisle*, 1900, ii, pp 186–202.
8 Ibid. ii p 189.
9 Ferrey, *Recollections*, Appendix, p 374.
10 Ibid, p 378.
11 Ibid, S Francis Xavier Church, Hereford, for the opening of which music was provided by the choir of St George's Church, Worcester, see Chapter 7, page 81; Elgar worshipped here during his residence in Hereford.
12 Scott, op cit, p 319.
13 Pugin, *Contrasts*, p 4.
14 Ibid, p 13.
15 Ibid, p 14.
16 In 1844 an article in the *British and Foreign Review* xxxiii, 1844, pp 115–116, was still able to contrast the fine singing at the Bavarian Embassy Chapel with the poverty and slovenliness of the music sung in St Paul's Cathedral.
17 Lambert, educated at Downside; active in local and national politics, free trade and sanitation being special concerns; 1854, first post-Reformation Mayor of Salisbury; gifted musician, well versed in ecclesiatical music of the Middle Ages; principal English exponent of Solesmes system of Plain Chant, member of Academy of St Cecilia, Rome; Gold medal from Pius ix for services to church music. Newman hoped that Lambert would 'come to hear our Gregorian Vespers in our new House' (4 July 1852).
18 Michael W Brooks, *John Ruskin and Victorian Architecture*, see p 33f., 'Chapel and Church: The religious background to architectural theory'.
19 *The Catholic Gentleman's Magazine*, [London], 1818, 'A Letter addressed to a Lady on Ancient and modern Music', p 57.
20 Isaac Willliams, educated at Trinity College, Oxford, friendly with Keble and Froude and curate to Newman, who dedicated *Church of the Fathers* (1840) to him; unsuccessful candidate for Professorship of Poetry. 1848–65, Incumbent of Stinchcombe.
21 see Sotheby's 'Netley Abbey' in *AR* 1791, p 111.
22 *Catholic Magazine and Review* ii, April 1832 , p 218.
23 Ibid, September 1832, pp 742–3.
24 *Catholic Magazine* iii, no xxx, July 1839, p 498.
25 Ibid. xxxi, August 1939, p 567.
26 Huddersfield, ibid, xxxii, September 1839, p 689.
27 Wilfrid Ward, *Life and Times of Cardinal Wiseman*,1897, I, p 356.
28 Preston, *Mus W* 1841, p 61.
29 Scott, *Lectures* p 319.
30 Pugin, *An Earnest Appeal* 1850, pp 3–5.

6 Music and Words

At the time of John Henry Newman's birth, in February 1801, there was, in England, a renewal of enthusiasm for an intellectual and aesthetic relationship with the European mainstream. This was by way of German Romanticism, the philosophy of Kant, and the music of Haydn and Mozart, which had come to challenge the long reign of Handelian oratorio. Orchestral music, supplied in the more important provincial centres by 'Gentlemen's Concerts' and Music Festivals, and in London by the Subscription Concerts promoted by Johann Peter Salomon, became fashionable. As it did so, private music-making tended away from glee-singing towards instrumental chamber music. By the turn of the century, while music by Haydn and Mozart was well established, that of Beethoven was generally unknown. The first performance of any of his chamber music was described by the indefatigable William Gardiner. In his diary he described how, in 1794, he took part in a performance of Beethoven's Trio for strings in E flat (Op.3). A manuscript score of this work had been brought to England from Bonn by an émigré priest – an ardent violinist – who was a guest of a Leicestershire lady with whom Gardiner was acquainted.[1] Five years later the first work of Beethoven to be published in London – *A Favourite Canzonetta, for the Piano Forte* (with words by William Wennington) – appeared. In 1805 a 'New Grand Symphony, never performed in England' by Beethoven was given at a New Musical Fund Concert. Taking part in that concert was George Smart, who during the next decade was to be the chief promoter of Beethoven's music in England. In 1813 the Philharmonic Society, of which Smart was a founder member, was founded and during its first season works by Beethoven were played at every performance. For John Henry Newman, who was very soon to become aware of his music, Beethoven was one of the most significant influences on his life.

Newman's enthusiasm for music was apparent early. It was suggested by his brother Francis that this was inherited from their father: 'The only

69

quality which I am aware that they had in common was – *love of music*'.[2]
John Henry had his first violin lessons at the age of ten, and he progressed
precociously, as his diary shows: 26 February 1811; 'began Music', 1–3
March; 'a lesson of music', 20 March; 'began a tune', 23 March; 'began
themes', and – a month later – 'began duets'.[3] The other notably musical
member of the family was Newman's second sister – named Jemima after
her mother – who was in the future to play the pianoforte more than
competently. John Henry also displayed an early enthusiasm for drama.
More than once during his schooldays he took part in miniature plays for
domestic production for which he provided music for the songs.

Francis Newman probably did his mother an injustice in omitting
mention of any interest in music on her part. For it was through her
attendance at a concert that John Henry's early interest in Beethoven was
first indicated. On 18 April, 1816, she wrote of going with a friend to an
orchestral concert at the King's Theatre, directed by Spagnoletti. The
programme included works by Haydn, Cherubini, Mozart and Beethoven.
They were 'fascinated by the Dutchman' and thought about 'you and your
musical party frequently'. Newman called Beethoven 'the Dutchman' to
plague his music master.[4] Not long after this he made a fair copy of sets of
fairly ambitious, if erratic, variations on French airs[5] which accompanied
him to Oxford when, in 1817, he took up a place at Trinity College. Here,
while his undergraduate academic record was less successful than had been
expected, he cultivated his literary and musical interests vigorously. In due
course he began to take some pride in his ability to achieve musical
correctness. In a follow-up letter of 31 March 1821 to his sister Jemima (in
whom, throughout his life, he especially confided the details of his musical
development) he announced his completion of a two-movement work for
violin and piano, which has not survived.

From the start he was much immersed in chamber music, and
throughout his university career belonged to some enthusiastic group of
musical protesters against a philistine climate.

There were times when music was almost too much of a good thing. On
3 June 1820 he wrote to his eldest sister, Harriet:

> I was asked by a man yesterday to go to his rooms for a *little* music at
> seven o'clock. I went. An old Don – a very good-natured man, but too fond
> of music – played Bass; and through his enthusiasm I was kept playing
> quartets on a heavy tenor from 7 to 12! O my poor arms and head and
> back.[6]

Two years later Newman's academic career took flight and he was
awarded a Fellowship at Oriel College. The fact that at the time of arrival
of the butler sent from Oriel to summon him to his new college, he was
practising the violin aroused serious doubts in the mind of the messenger

regarding Newman's suitability for promotion.[7] Despite the butler's reservations, however, a catholic taste for music was notably part of the lives of many whose spiritual direction was to be similar to that taken by Newman. It was shortly before he was ordained as deacon in 1824 that he had a lively letter from a friend, John William Bowden, a cellist. The contents he immediately communicated to Jemima:

> ... He tells me that Sola, his sister's music master, brought Rossini to dine in Grosv[enor]. Place not long since – and that as far as they could judge (for he does not speak English) he is as unassuming and obliging man as ever *breathed*! only think he seemed as highly pleased with *every thing* and desirous of making himself agreeable. Laboring, indeed, under a very severe cold he did not sing; but he accompanied two or three of his own songs etc. in the most brilliant manner, giving the Piano the effect of an Orchestra – nay *three* Orchestras, I say Eleanor *it was*! As became in a *private* not a professional way, Bowden called on him – and found him surrounded in a low dark room by 8 or 9 Italians, all screaming *macaw* (o[nly] th[ink]! and of Mad. Colbran Rossini in a dirty gown and her hair in curl papers, made such a clamour that he was glad to escape as fast as he could.[8]

In 1826 Joseph Blanco White, a former Catholic priest and a convert to Anglicanism, became a member of the Oriel Common Room. A dedicated violinist, his veneration of Beethoven gained Newman's ready collaboration in chamber music performance. On an occasion reported by J B Mozley, professional assistance came from Alexander Reinagle, son of the celebrated cellist, Joseph Reinagle:

> With Reinagle, Newman [viola] and Blanco White had frequent [trios] at the latter's lodgings, where I was all the audience .... Most interesting it was to contrast Blanco White's excited and indeed agitated countenance with Newman's sphinx-like immobility, as the latter drew long rich notes with a steady hand.[9]

Others of Newman's acquaintance – all Fellows of their colleges – who were regular companions in chamber music included Frederick Rogers, also of Oriel, William Donkin, of St Edmund Hall, and George Rowden, of New College. Rowden was remembered as 'one of the best double bass players in England'.[10]

As well as undertaking tutorial duties at Oriel, and pursuing his researches into church history and theology, Newman undertook the duties of curate at St Clement's Church in Oxford. In 1828 he became vicar of the University Church of St Mary the Virgin, where across the next fifteen years he delivered the sermons that established his reputation as a great preacher. As an undergraduate, William Ewart Gladstone – the other great orator of the age – heard Newman preach.

'Taking the man as a whole,' he remembered, 'there was a stamp and seal upon him; there was a solemn music and sweetness in the tone'.

Further, he said, 'I do not believe that there has been anything like his influence in Oxford, when it was at its height, since Abelard lectured in Paris.[11]

The pertinence of music to religious philosophy was briefly explored in the eighteenth century by the Irish philosopher George Berkeley. In *Principles of Human Knowledge* he wrote of

> ... certain ideas, of I know not what sort, in the mind of God, which are so many marks of notes, that direct Him to produce sensations in our minds, in a constant and regular method: much after the same manner, as a musician is directed by the notes of music, to produce that harmonious train and composition of sound, which is called a tune; tho' they who hear the music do not perceive the notes, and may be intirely ignorant of them.[12]

Berkeley's train of thought runs in a direction taken by Newman in an extended argument in his sermon 'Moral Consequences of Single Sins', commenced by consideration of 'the seven notes of the scale':

> ... yet is it possible that the inexhaustible evolution and disposition of notes, so rich yet so simple, so intricate yet so regulated, so varied yet so majestic, should be a mere sound, which is gone and perishes? Can it be that those mysterious stirrings of heart, and keen emotions, and strange yearnings after we know not whence, should be wrought in us by what is unsubstantial, and comes and goes, and begins and ends in itself? It is not so; it cannot be. No; they have escaped from some higher sphere; they are the outpourings of eternal harmony in the medium of created sound.[13]

This theme, of relationship between ideas, words and music frequently appears in Newman's thinking – in an absolute form in his own exercises in setting words to music. These settings (see pp. 92–93) testify also to the spreading influence of hymns within both Methodism and the Church of England. Within the latter a new order of hymn composition was initiated by Reginald Heber, sometime Fellow of All Souls, and John Keble. The verses of Heber, who became Bishop of Calcutta, are colourful, vigorous, and sturdily missionary. Keble – a Tutor at Oriel from 1811 until 1823 – from 1831 for ten years was Professor of Poetry at Oxford. In 1827 he published anonymously two volumes of *Thoughts in Verse for the Sundays and Holy Days throughout the Year*. These pieces of pastoral distillation relate on the one hand to the gentle and appropriately pastoral vision of George Herbert, on the other to the persuasive influence of Wordsworth. There was also a debt to the Fathers of the Early Church, exemplified in a singularly affecting translation from St Basil, 'Hail gladenning light'.

In his essay on *Sacred Poetry* of 1825 Keble instructed his readers as follows:

> ... It is required, we apprehend, in all poets, but particularly in sacred poets, that they should seem to write with a view of unburthening their

minds, and not for the sake of writing; for love of the subject, not of the employment.[14]

Through his preaching, his scholarship, and his contributions to the *Tracts for the Times* which distinguished the Tractarian, or Oxford Movement, in the Church of England, Keble exercised a profound influence. Newman, indeed, described him as the 'true and primary author of the Oxford Movement.'

Newman – known generally by some two or three poems – was at times under as much psychological compulsion in respect of poetry as often he was in prose. He took Keble's advice and was often eager, if not anxious, to set out his thoughts in this medium. This was particularly the case at times of crisis. Most of his themes were sacred; but not all.

Any Miltonic aspirations were ended with a schoolboy fragment 'On Music', grandly addressed to the 'Soul of the World'. Some early poems had a charm which came, and went, and later in life reappeared. 'Solitude' 1816; 'Snapdragon (A Riddle for a Flower Book)' 1827; and 'The Trance of Time' 1827; make a set of evocative family pieces. 'Opusculum' (1829) 'for a very small album' is a model of economy and good humour.

> Fair Cousin, thy page
> is small to encourage
> the thoughts which engage
> The mind of a sage
>   such as I am
>
> 'Twere in teaspoon to take
> the whole Genovese lake,
> or a lap-dog to make
> the white Elephant sac
>   —cred in Siam

In 1824 Newman first came face to face with death – the death of his father. During the next year his father's mother died. In those days such events came in family life with menacing regularity. At the beginning of 1828 the Newman family was devastated by the sudden, unexpected, death of Mary, the youngest girl of the family. During her last brief illness she had, Newman informed Keble, been comforted by reciting poems from *The Christian Year*. A few months after her death Newman wrote 'Consolations in Bereavement' – a delicate, hopeful, reverent valediction.

During the following year Newman had an opportunity critically to consider the nature and function of both poetry and music. Blanco White, editing a new magazine, the *London Review*, invited two contributions from Newman: one, 'with reference to Aristotle's Poetics', to be on poetry, the other on music. The first was duly published, although the second did not appear – the magazine, according to Newman, dying of dullness after its second issue. The high view of music held by Newman is powerfully apparent in the essay that did appear. 'We may', he wrote,

> . . . liken the Greek drama to the music of the Italian school; in which the wonder is, how so much richness of invention in detail can be accommodated to a style so simple and uniform. Each is the development of grace, fancy, pathos, and taste, in the respective media of representation and sound.[15]

Before long he was to become acquainted with the music of the Italian school, which he here so elegantly invoked.

In the late summer of 1832, waiting on critical reaction to his first scholarly book, *The Arians of the Fourth Century*, Newman was in a state of exhaustion. He recalled how, from his reading of the lives and influence of the Alexandrian philosophers Clement and Origen, it seemed that 'some portions of their teaching came like music to my inward ear'.[16] So he must take refuge in the practice of music – always, during periods of tension, his refreshment. On 7 September he wrote into a music manuscript book inherited from his father a song 'To my sister Harriett', of which an extract is shown in plate 6.

On 4 October Newman wrote to Hurrell Froude, a pupil and intimate friend of Keble, now a Fellow of Oriel who shared the duties of tutor with Newman:

> Oxford has not yet begun to fill. I have been entirely idle the last month. The Violin has been my only care – and, tho' I have not practised or progressed much, yet I see that I could easily play better than ever I did, and with *regular* attention might do what I pleased.[17]

Newman's friendship with Hurrell Froude brought him closer to Keble, an association which greatly hastened the progress of the Tractarian Movement. 'Well', said Froude, 'if I was asked what good deed I have ever done, I should say I had brought Keble and Newman to understand each other'.[18] As the end of the year approached, Newman was grateful to be able to look forward to sharing a holiday in the Mediterranean arranged by Froude's father for the benefit of his son's health. Hurrell Froude suffered from, and was prematurely to die of, tuberculosis. In November, mindful of the effectiveness of Keble's *Christian Year*, Newman and Froude began to plan a series of poems for *The British Magazine*, as an instrument for promoting their concept of the nature of the Church. A tentative title for the project was *Lyra Apostolica*.

In anticipation of a period for reflection, Newman prepared himself to confide his feelings into a new exercise book, inscribed 'J.H. Newman / Oriel College / 'non lusisse pudet' [I am not ashamed to have played]'. It was dated 16 November, 1832, and almost immediately put to use. Pieces were inscribed on November 18, 20 and 21, 22, 23 (two), 25 (two) in Oxford, 28 and 29 in Iffley, and on 2 December in Oxford. As written, pieces were marked off – a stroke of the pen for each – within these categories: 'Sonnets (10), Common Metre (13), Sixes (1), Long & Shorts (5), Extra-ordinarius (8)'.

During his absence from England Newman, in two creative spasms, wrote a sequence of poems which, all in all, constitutes a spiritual diary. On 13 December, the boat now lying off Lisbon, he wrote 'Siren isles' on which Geoffrey Faber commented, 'Some sound of music must have travelled poignantly across the water, as they passed Lisbon and he wrote his tale of verses for the day'.[19] At Malta, where the passengers were disallowed from landing on account of the fear of cholera, Newman describes to Harriet 'the most miserable Christmas Day I conceive it to be my lot to suffer. On 26 December, after a troubled night, he wrote the poem published in *Lyra Apostolica* as 'Sleep'. In the collected *Verses on Various Occasions* of 1867 the title was changed to 'Sleeplessness'. A number of other equally significant changes took place, some – such as 'Dreams', written at Paestum on 26 February – relating to themes exposed in *The Dream of Gerontius*.

The travels of Newman and his companions are detailed in the poems of the winter and spring of 1832–33.

Newman was in Rome in 1833, during Holy Week, when he made it his duty to meet the Abbé Fortunato Santini, music librarian of the Vatican. He was anxious to catch up with those – in England, mostly zealous high churchmen with musicological and /or antiquarian interests – eager to cultivate Gregorian chant. On 17 March 1833 he wrote to Samuel Francis Wood, one of his pupils at Oriel:

> I am making some attempt, while here, to inquire into the history of the Gregorian Chants but fear it will come to nothing. The greater part of the Music can be got in England, and as for dates and changes I suspect the Italians know little or nothing about them. I am to see Angelo Mari (March 18) this morning, and learn from him if any books in the Vatican will throw light on the subject. And I have got acquainted with an abbé, a very agreeable well informed man who has great hoards of old music. I feel very much my want of knowledge, on the subject – for tho' I am very fond of music, I am very unlearned in it, having had little opportunity to become acquainted with it as a language.[20]

On Easter Day, 7 April, he wrote to Henry Jenkyns, a Fellow of Oriel,

> This last week we have heard the celebrated Miserere, or rather the two Misereres – for there are two compositions by Allegri and Bai[n]i, so like each other that the performers themselves can scarcely tell the difference between them – one is performed on the Thursday and the other on Good Friday – The voices are certainly very surprising – there is no instrument to support them – but they have the art of continuing their notes so long and equally, that the effect is as if an organ were playing, or rather an organ of violin strings, for the notes are clearer, more subtle and piercing, and the

more impassioned (so to say) than those of an organ – The music itself is doubtless very fine – as everyone says – but I found myself unable to understand all parts of it – here and there it was extremely fine – but it is impossible to understand such a composition on once or twice hearing – in it's [*sic*] style it is more like Corelli's music than any other I know (though very different too) and this is not wonderfull, as Corelli was Master of the Pope's Chapel; and so, educated in the school of Allegri, Palestrina, and the rest.[21]

While in Rome Newman and Froude visited Nicholas Wiseman at the English College, after which the Froudes returned home. This left Newman free to fulfil his wish again to visit Sicily. He was not sorry, he wrote on 6 April, to go alone – 'in order, as Wordsworth would say, to commune with high nature'.[22] During this second visit, accompanied by a Neapolitan servant, Newman was taken seriously ill in Castro Giovanni. So severe was the fever that he came to think that he would not recover. Mark Pattison recollected in his notes what Newman remembered:

> Priest came to see him, but he was not in a state to have any conversation; people dying all around and bells tolling continually for them; people of the house thought the heretic couldn't hear the bells; was given over for a week. First place he went to, on getting better, the cathedral – old Norman; might have fancied himself in England. Left C[astro] G[iovanni] so weak he could not walk; when he got to Palermo people considered him dying; sea-air restored him.[23]

Towards the end of May, recovered from the fever – but weak and nervously exhausted – Newman could only bring himself back to a settled state of mind by recollecting what Wiseman had said to him and Froude when they were in Rome. To his servant, perplexed by Newman's depression, he repeated Wiseman's words: 'I have a work to do in England'.[24]

For three weeks the boat on which he was travelling, on the first stage of his homeward journey, to Marseilles, was left becalmed in Palermo. During this period, undisturbed, he gave himself to poetry, at the rate of one poem a day over the next month. On 16 June, the day on which the voyage recommenced, he wrote 'The Pillar of the Cloud' ('Lead, kindly light'), termed by J H Muirhead 'the marching song of the Tractarian movement'. He added, 'surely never a hymn that came more directly out of the heart; perhaps none that goes more directly to it.[25]

Six days later – also at sea – 'Death', later titled *Hora novissima*, after a hymn by Bernard of Morlaix,[26] and on 27 June 'Waiting for Christ' were written. After the death of Hurrell Froude on 28 February 1836, twelve lines were added to this poem, which was then given the title, 'Separation of Friends'. Of the poems of this period, 'Waiting for Christ' shows Newman in a mood of deep tranquillity. Subsequently headed 'Refrigerium', the poem illustrates the 'flowery place' where are the waiting souls of Bede's pastoral vision in the Fifth Book of his *Ecclesiastical History*.[27]

Newman's passage from Anglicanism to Catholicism was accomplished in stages. Music, in which so much of his spiritual apperception was placed, was inevitably an instrument in that process. In 1836, the year in which both Hurrell Froude and his mother died, a new church for the village of Littlemore – which was within the Oxford parish of St Mary-the-Virgin – was being built. The ground had been made available by Oriel College, which had also helped with funds towards the building costs, to which Newman made his own contribution. Increasingly Newman came to find Littlemore a place of refuge. His involvement in the life of the little community led him to using his musical and his pedagogic skills, which are reflected in a note written to his sister Jemima (now Mrs Mozley) on 1 April 1840. He was teaching the village children to sing 'some new [hymn-]tunes, as well as experimenting with Gregorian chant'. He had found a violin and that was helpful.[28]

At Littlemore Newman made much use of *A Collection of Psalms and Hynn Tunes, Chants and other Music* compiled for the use of St Peter's Church, Oxford, and introduced by the vicar, Walter Kerr Hamilton, Fellow of Merton College and a future Bishop of Salisbury. The book was published in 1840. Hamilton, a high churchman, was greatly concerned with improving the standard of music in parish churches. The musical editor of the book (which remains at Littlemore) was Newman's sometime chamber music companion, A R Reinagle, who was for thirty years organist of the parish church of St Peter in the East. The collection contained within small space a considerable variety: Gregorian chants, arranged by G V Cox 'without any alteration of the character and peculiar modulation . . .'; German chorales suggested by Baron von Bunsen, Prussian Ambassador in London; and some original tunes, including Reinagle's 'St Peter', which remains in general use.

In 1842 he leased a row of cottages in Littlemore, which became a centre where men in sympathy with his ideas came to live in community. It was a testing time, and it was here that his transition to Catholicism was painfully achieved. In 1843 he resigned his living at St Mary-the-Virgin: 'The Parting of Friends', the sermon preached at Littlemore on 29 September, marking the end of one phase of his career.

A period of reflection, in which Newman considered his position, and during which several of his friends were converted to Catholicism, ended in 1845. On 3 October he resigned his Fellowship at Oriel College, and six days later he was received into the Catholic Church by Father Dominic Barberi, an Italian Passionist priest brought to St Mary's College, Oscott, by Wiseman. After his confirmation by Wiseman at Oscott on 1 November, Newman considered Wiseman's proposals for his future sphere of activity. These contained the idea of a secular priesthood within a community dedicated to pastoral work, education and scholarship. For this purpose Wiseman proposed making use of the old buildings at Oscott – which had been replaced by the new college of 1839 – where Newman, with those who had associated themselves with him, would undertake that work after a period of further study in Rome. The source of inspiration was the Oratorian ideal of St Philip Neri.

Newman travelled to Rome with Ambrose St John, formerly a pupil of Keble, who was to remain a lifelong friend. After a period of preparation at the College of Propaganda and an interview with Pope Pius IX, the establishment of an Oratory in England came a step nearer to realization. On 14 March, with St John and Robert Coffin (who was also to join the Oratorian community), Newman attended mass and communicated at St Peter's tomb. At breakfast they met Robert Berkeley, of Spetchley Park, Worcestershire, a former student at Oscott who in the future was to become acquainted with Edward Elgar.[29] At the end of May Newman and St John were ordained to the priesthood in the Church of St John Lateran. Until their return to England at the end of the year they remained in Italy. Some part of the time was spent in further preparation for their future as Oratorians, and some in sightseeing.

During that summer Newman received a copy of a novel with the provocative title 'From Oxford to Rome and how it has fared with some of those who lately made the journey. By a Companion Traveller'. The author, a Miss Elizabeth Harris, had been a convert to Rome who retracted and went back to the Church of England. It was likely, she suggested, that Newman and his followers were also at the point of similar return. Although ill-written, factually inaccurate, and abusive, Newman recognized that the case required an answer. He decided that this could most effectively be done through the same fictional medium. The result was *Loss and Gain*, an 'intelligible and exact representation of the thoughts, sentiments, and aspirations' prevalent in Oxford in the 1840s.[30] The title of the novel was taken from 'The Parent Church', one of the poems of December 1832. In this quasi-autobiographical work, in acknowledging self-doubt and questioning the foundations of belief, Newman was breaking new ground in fiction. In form it is a sequence of interwoven dialogues which represent the nature of Newman's own spiritual development towards the climax of his conversion. The dialogue is shared between Charles Reding, in character shown to be near to Newman himself, and a variety of representative Oxford men.

There are two points in the book at which music becomes significant. When, during a country walk they visited an Anglo-Catholic chapel, Reding and his friend William Sheffield were brought to discussion of the subject of imagery. Sheffield disapproved of such, protesting that there were those who said, 'that we ought to put up crucifixes by the wayside, in order to excite religious feeling'. Reding reminded him that such representations can have a similar effect as music. 'Do *you* like music' asked Sheffield. Reding replied, 'You ought to know whom I have so often frightened with my fiddle'. At a later point, there is a long discussion of the merits of Classical as opposed to Gothic architecture, and at the same time of Gregorian chant and 'modern music' and their suitability for worship. When one disputant suggests that 'if he had his will, there should be no architecture in the English churches but Gothic, and no music but Gregorian', Reding says that, 'all these adjuncts of worship, whether music or architecture, were national, they were the mode in which religious feeling showed itself in particular times and places'.

In real life the contest between Roman and English, Classical and Gothic was between Wiseman and Pugin.

Notes

1   An eccentric letter from Gardiner to Beethoven (BL Add MS 27900), Jonathan Wildshere, *William Gardiner of Leicester (1770–1853)*, Leicester 1970, p 16.
2   *John Francis Newman, Contributions chiefly to the Early History of the late Cardinal Newman . . .*, London, p 7.
3   LD I, p 9.
4   LD I, p 19, fn.
5   Oratory Library, MS dated 12 October 1816.
6   LD I, 3 June 1820.
7   Newman, *Autobiographical Writings*, pp 61–62.
8   LD I 3 March 1824, p 173.
9   Mozley, *Letters*, p 95.
10 Rogers became a distinguished public servant and was created Lord Blachford; Donkin the Savilian Professor of Astronomy at Oxford; Rowden, a clergyman, Precentor of Chichester Cathedral.
11 Reid, *Life of Gladstone*, pp 203–4.
12 Berkeley, George, *Principles of Human Knowledge*, ed T E Jessop, London 1945, p 69.
13 'The Theory of Development in Religious Doctrines' (1843), *Fifteen Sermons Preached before the University of Oxford 1826–1843*, Rivingtons, London, New Edition 1884, pp 346–7.
14 Keble, 'Sacred Poetry', *English Critical Essays (XIX Century)*, Oxford 1916/1929, p 199.
15 Newman, 'Poetry', ibid, p 228.
16 *Apologia pro Vita Sua*, Reprint of First edition etc ed John Gamble, London [1913] 2 vols I, p 70.
17 LD III 1832, p 99.
18 Church, R W, *The Oxford Movement*, Macmillan, London 1891, p 271.
19 Faber, Geoffrey, *Oxford Apostles*, Faber & Faber, London 1953, p 265.
20 LD III, letter to S F Wood (ob 1843), p 255.

21   LD III, 7 April 1833, p 279; Rev H E W Goddard (1792?–1878), a Sussex clergyman also visited Santini at about the same time and collected many valuable works, now in BL.

22   Ker, JHN, 1990, p 70.

23   Pattison, *Memoirs*, p 196 f.; the likelihood is that Newman was suffering from malaria, at that time particularly prevalent in Mediterranean countries.

24   *Apologia* I, p 29.

25   Muirhead, *Nine Famous Birmingham Men*, p 201.

26   Horatio Parker (1863–1919), American composer and a friend of Elgar, selected words from the poem *De Contempu Mundi* of Bernard of Cluny (12th century) for the text of his oratorio, *Hora novissima*, performed at the Three Choirs Festival at Worcester in 1899. The words *Hora novissima* in the original poem preface a hymn on the subject of the Last Judgment. Three years later Parker's oratorio *St Christopher* was performed at the Worcester Festival.

27   *Hist Book* V, Chapter XII, Everyman Edition, p 245. Elgar's setting of this poem, 'They are at rest', was composed for the opening of the Royal Mausoleum at Windsor on 22 January 1910 on the anniversary of the death of Queen Victoria.

28   Jemima m John Mozley, printer of Derby in 1836, Anne Mozley, ed., *Letters and Correspondence of John Henry Newman during his Life in the English Church*, London 1891, 2 vols, II, p 67.

29   Robert Berkeley (1823–1897, ed Oscott College and in Rome, m 1851, settled at Spetchley, 'widely and deeply respected, the central figure of the county and prominent in Worcester': *The Discourses Preached at the Funeral of Mr Robert Berkeley*, September 1897.

30   Newman, S H, *Loss and Gain*, OUP 1986, p 195 f.

7   A Catholic Upbringing

The earliest entries in the records of the Catholic parish in Worcester were made in 1685,[1] but it was not until 1827 that it became possible to consider building a chapel adequate to the needs of a growing congregation. In spite of the fact that in 1829, in Worcester – as elsewhere in the Midlands – there was much opposition to the Act of Toleration, St George's Chapel was built and ceremonially opened on Thursday 16 July. Mass was celebrated by Bishop Walsh, who was assisted by Dr Weedall, president of Oscott. W H Sharman, well known throughout the Midlands, directed the music. This consisted of extracts from various works by Handel, Haydn and Mozart, performed by choir and orchestra. As was generally the case, musicians were employed irrespective of personal religious commitment; so among the solo singers was William Machin, a lay clerk from Lichfield Cathedral, well known across the Midlands. Weedall, who preached at morning and afternoon services, was praised by the newspaper for using 'the most liberal and conciliatory language', and for admonishing 'his Catholic brethren to bear with patience those calumnies and misrepresentations under which they might labour, and to overcome by their exemplary lives, fervently praying for the conversion of their calumniators'.[2] In the Guide for the City of Worcester the new chapel was given a note of approval which, however, cannot refrain from suggesting Catholics to be something of a race apart.

> The present elegant building, erected at the bottom of Sansome Street in the year 1829, abundantly attests the improved state of public feeling, and of the laws, in reference to these people.[3]

The first organist and choir-master at St George's was a Mr Beresford. It was under his successor, Mr C Baldwyn, however, that the choir gained more than a local reputation, so that in 1839, together with assorted instrumentalists, it was required to perform at the opening of the chapel in Hereford, which – like St George's served by Jesuit priests – so infuriated Pugin.[4]

The fact that on Baldwyn's retirement in 1846 the vacancy was talked about as far away as Cheltenham[5] symbolized his achievement in creating a strong musical tradition. The successful candidate was William Henry Elgar, then aged 20, who on the recommendation of his employer, the London publishing house of Coventry and Hollier, had come to Worcester in the previous year as piano tuner, with the intention of establishing himself as a general musical practitioner. He played piano, organ and violin, and in due course – with a music-dealing business in the High Street – in more ways than one was at the centre of the musical life of the community.

When William Elgar was settling into his post of organist, another young man, William Done, was two years into his task of restoring the fortunes of music in the Cathedral. For seven years he had been apprentice and then assistant to the noticeably undistinguished Charles Clarke. After Done had conducted his first Three Choirs Festival in 1845 the *Worcester Berrows Journal* complimented 'him for the unusual firmness and ability displayed by him as conductor'. He was to remain in office for half a century and to prove a beneficial influence to younger musicians.

In 1848 William Elgar married Anne Greening, of Handley in Herefordshire. In 1850 a son, Henry John was born, and in May 1852 a daughter named Lucy. She was the first of the Elgar children to be baptized at St George's, this ceremony taking place on 26 May 1853. By this time Anne Elgar had been received into the Catholic Church. William remained Protestant.

In 1855 another daughter, Susanna Maria was born, and two years later Edward William, who was baptised at St George's on 11 June.[6] The godparents were William and Caroline Leicester, friends and neighbours of the Elgars, whose two-year old son, Hubert, was to become Edward's lifelong friend. On 29 August 1859 the youngest of the Elgar sons, Frederic Joseph ('Jo') was baptized at St George's.

As were all children in former times, young Edward Elgar was acquainted with the facts of mortality (and hope of immortality) early in life. William Leicester died in 1860. On 10 May 1864 the funeral took place of Henry John, aged fourteen, the eldest child of the Elgar family, and on 8 September 1866 that of his brother, Jo; both had contracted scarlet fever – then, for children, a deadly disease. All were buried in the cemetery allowed to St George's.[7] As a remembrance of his brother Jo, Edward was given by Father Waterworth, the parish priest, an engraving of the Death of St Joseph, inscribed with 'Jesus, Mary, Joseph, Pray for me in my own agony', the prayer later to have its place in *The Dream of Gerontius*. Jo's funeral took place immediately before the Three Choirs Festival in Worcester, in which, as usual, William Elgar played the violin.

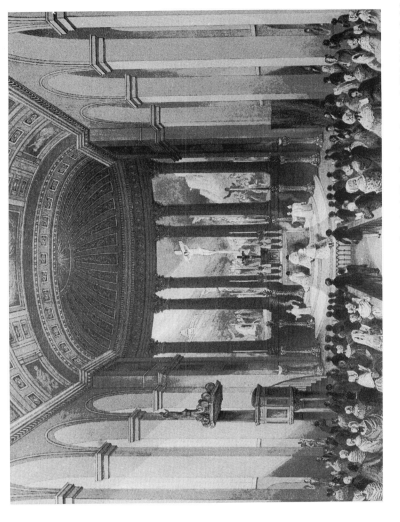

1 'Celebration of Easter Mass in Moorfields Chapel on Easter Sunday' *The London Journal*, Vol. I, No. 2, March 8, 1845

3   Mount St. Bernard's Abbey
    from *An Apology for the Revival . . . 1843*

2   St. George's Cathedral

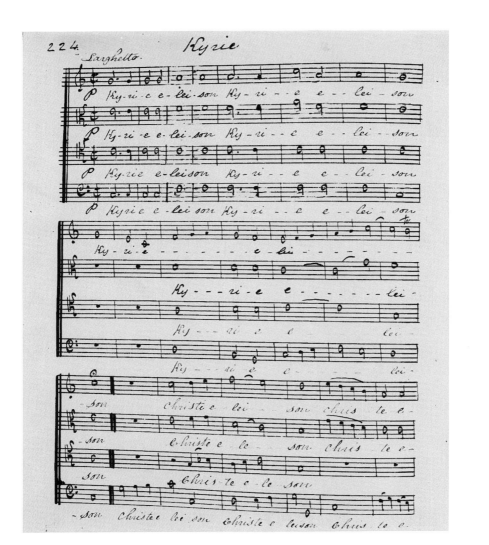

4 'Kyrie' from Webbe's Mass in C arranged for Four Voices by John
Robinson 1816

Dreams

Oh miserable power
To dreams allowed, to raise the guilty past,
And back a while the illumined spirit to cast
On its youth's twilight hours;
In mockery guiling it to act again
The revel or the scoff in Satan's frantic train!

Nay, hush thee, angry heart!
It seems all high toned grief a penitent,
Take patiently thy thorn divinely sent —
Its profitable smart
Shall pierce thee in thy virtue's palmy home,
And warn thee what thou art, & whence thy wealth has come.
Road from Pæstum to Salerno.

Febr. 26. 1833

5   'Dreams'

6 Refrigerium: 'They are at rest'

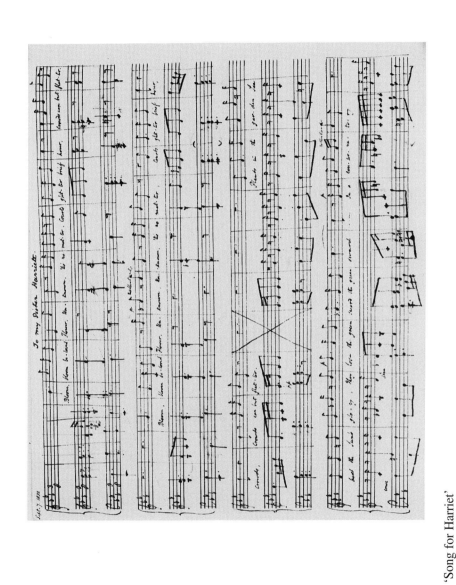

7 'Song for Harriet'

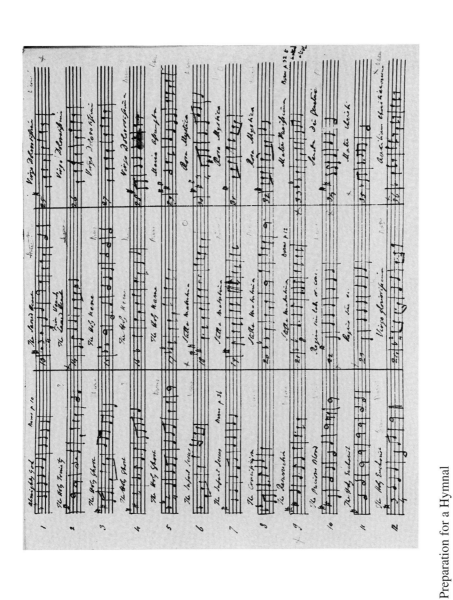

8   Preparation for a Hymnal

9   West End of Netley Abbey, Thomas Walmsley (1763–1805/6)

10 'Baptizatus est Edwardus Guglielmus filius Guglielmi Henrici Elgar & Annae Elgar . . .'. Baptismal certificate

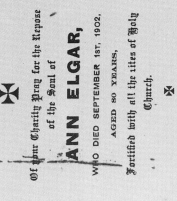

Of your Charity Pray for the Repose

of the Soul of

ANN ELGAR,

WHO DIED SEPTEMBER 1ST, 1902,

AGED 80 YEARS,

Fortified with all the rites of Holy

Church.

"On whose Soul sweet Jesus have mercy."

PRAYER.

Absolve, we beseech Thee, O Lord, the soul of Thy servant ANN, that being dead to the world she may live to Thee, and the sins she has committed in this life through human frailty, do Thou of Thy most merciful goodness forgive, through Jesus Christ our Lord. Amen.

Eternal rest give unto her O Lord, and let perpetual light shine upon her.

LE JOUR DE LA DÉLIVRANCE
Tous les jours il approche

(Ven. columba.)

Le plaisir de mourir sans peine
vaut bien la peine de vivre sans plaisir
Oh qu'elle est heureuse! Elle commence à jouir
quand tant d'autres commencent à pleurer

Ch. Lesueille   Pl. 323   à Paris

11 In Memoriam Anne Elgar

12   The woods at Birchwood, 'H.F.B. 1911'

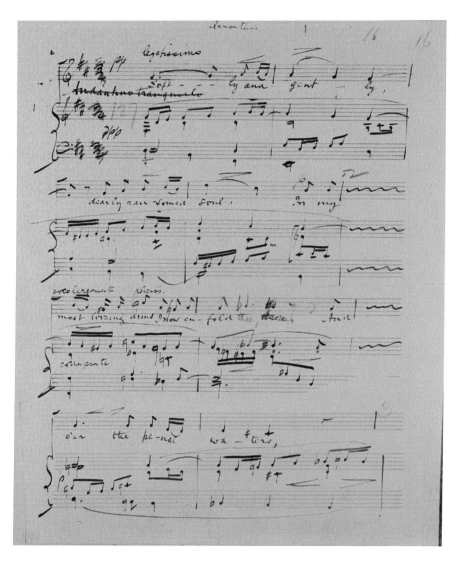

13   'Softly and gently', the end of The Dream of Gerontius

Edward was allowed into one rehearsal to hear, for the first time, Beethoven's Mass in C.

Father Waterworth was a priest and a scholar of some distinction. Educated at Stonyhurst and in Rome he served as a teacher for some years, first in a Jesuit grammar school in London, and then at Stonyhurst. His first parish experience followed in Hereford, in charge of the church of which Pugin had spoken so disparagingly. In 1854 Waterworth became rector of the Jesuit Church in Farm Street, London, where he was confessor to the recently converted Henry Edward Manning. In 1858 he came to Worcester as 'Rector of the College of St George', to remain in that office for twenty years, during which he continued to publish scholarly works on church history. By reason of his office and his reputation he was an important influence on Catholic education.

Edward Elgar was taught entirely by Catholic teachers. First, in Britannia Square, in a school – mainly for girls, but with infant boys – kept by Miss Caroline Walsh. This was followed by a period in the school at Spetchley, near Worcester, which was given by Robert Berkeley[8] in 1841 and built to a design by Pugin. The teaching was in the hands of the Sisters of St Paul. The distance of four miles from Worcester would have made daily journeys impracticable, thus it may be supposed that during the week Edward was boarded locally. Of his schooldays at Spetchley he retained one particular memory, which he repeated to the music critic, Ernest Newman:

> Elgar told me that as a boy he used to gaze from the school windows in rapt wonder at the great trees in the park swaying in the wind, and he pointed to a passage in *Gerontius* in which he had recorded in music his subconscious memories of them.[9]

> The sound is like the rushing of the wind –
> The summer wind among the lofty pines,
> Swelling and dying, echoing round about,
> Now here, now distant, wild and beautiful.

The trees at Spetchley were part of an old forest that had stretched from Worcester to Evesham. while the elm avenue was said to have been planted in the seventeenth century by one of the Berkeleys described by the diarist John Evelyn as 'a most ingenious, virtuous & religious Gent: seated near *Worster* [sic], & very cunning in Gardening &c.'[10].

Edward's schooling took place during a period of impending major changes in education. Not yet compulsory, such general education as was available was conducted in schools of the 'National Society for Promoting the Education of the Poor in the Principles of the Established Church'. More privileged boys were, in due course, sent to anciently endowed Grammar Schools, or to certain Public Schools. The sons of the Catholic aristocracy attended schools which came into being with the repatriated seminarians at the end of the eighteenth century. Schools which were established for the sons of Catholics who had prospered in commerce in some larger towns were sometimes fortunate to have educational opportunities provided by teachers who understood what was required to provide a good foundation to a commercial or a legal career. As in Sedgeley Park, stress was laid on reading and writing and commercial arithmetic, with geography, some Latin, perhaps French, and religion. Mr Francis Reeve maintained such an Academy at Grove Villa, Rainbow Hill, Worcester from about 1860, and afterwards at Littleton House, Lower Wick, until 1890.

In place of religious instruction from the clergy of the Church of England, for Catholic boys in Worcester there was the more colourful and more dogmatic teaching of the clergy of St George's. The church itself, being in a continuing process of beautification, supplemented any other aesthetic instruction. There is no reason to believe that the education provided for Edward Elgar here was in any way inferior to that of any other school in Worcester. He was at school altogether for ten years, benefiting from a longer period of education than many of his contemporaries. Attendance at a Catholic school in England, however, could lead to a sense of alienation. As was the case within living memory in the early years of this century, boys at such schools were regarded by their contemporaries – under parental influence – with a degree of suspicion. Elgar – not only in youth – was sensitive, subject to moods of withdrawal, and often misunderstood.

Musically he was more fortunate than most. He was making progress with the violin. He had the run of the stock of music in his father's shop. There was amateur music-making on a scale difficult in modern times to comprehend, and preparations – which spread from one to another of the three participating cities – for the Three Choirs Festival. For some years prior to the completion of a major programme of restoration in 1874, however, the regular functions of the cathedral were much disturbed. Apart from the special occasions during Festival time, the music at St George's was then more various than that in the cathedral. Although Elgar himself claimed to have looked at some of the part-books shown to him by Done, Done himself was somewhat indifferent to their contents, as his daughter described:

> With the advent of Modern Music the anthems and services by the Old Masters were less often sung and it has been said by musicians that the manner of rendering them is a lost art.[11]

At St George's the music library of the church contained two sets of books published in 1792 (presumably Webbe's two *Collections*) as well as a selection of 'elaborate Motets for use at the Offertory and Benediction' published by Vincent Novello. Such music – the regular experience of the young Elgar – was in the Embassy chapel tradition. So far as the more garish, operatic style pieces that were sung, there was sometimes the pleasure of hearing them performed by visiting singers who were appearing otherwise in performances at the theatre.

In July 1872 Edward entered the adult world. With the benefit of commercial training in Francis Reeve's Academy he became a clerk in the office of William Allen, a Catholic lawyer with rooms in Sansome Place. For the first time – on 14 July – he played the organ for Mass in St George's.

The time had not yet come when all musical needs could be supplied off the peg. In a cathedral, or an ambitious church – as in the case of Robinson in York – the organist was frequently called upon to exercise composerly skills. Apart from his wider interests in secular orchestral experience, Edward learned to write voice parts into classical instrumental works for performance at St George's. Because he was a fine violinist, and had an unerring sense of the effective placing of musical sounds, the result was that the end products carried a stamp of authenticity. To the congregational ear, they resembled tolerably well the sacred works of those composers whose sonatas and symphonies he plundered for this purpose. Notable examples were Mozart's Sonata for violin and pianoforte (K 547) into which a setting of the Gloria was placed, and sections from Beethoven's Fifth, Seventh and Ninth symphonies which accommodated a somewhat extended *Credo*.

The early works composed for St George's did not go so far as to suggest that there was within them the makings of a great composer. They were practicable, showing understanding of melodic structure, tolerant of harmonic proprieties, and – in their situation – appropriate to an occasion. It was, of course, a great advantage to the young Elgar to be able to put his music to the test of public performance. Among the earliest extant works is a *Kyrie*[12] in three sections, probably written in 1876. For three voices (no alto), it displays some subtlety in the treatment of the motifs which run throughout.

On 29 June 1879 the fiftieth anniversary of the opening of St George's was commemorated. At the morning service Haydn's second Mass was performed with orchestral accompaniment. At Vespers there were works by popular European composers – Anfossi, Spohr, Winter and Hummel – and Vincent Novello's *Infant's Prayer* and 'E Elgar's *Tantum ergo*'.[13]

A year later, on 7 June, a new chancel, side chapels, baptistry and sacristy were opened. A new high altar was given by Mr Tyler of Mealcheapen Street, and a new altar for St Joseph's chapel by Major Robert Berkeley.

Ex. 14

Kyrie

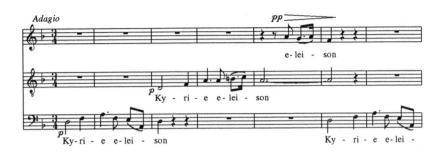

At high mass Hummel in B flat was performed with complete orchestral accompaniment, Mr Ed W Elgar being leader of the band, and Mr [W H] Elgar presiding at the organ. The sermon was preached by the Right Reverend Dr Ullathorne, Bishop of Birmingham.

At vespers a solo from Pergolesi was 'beautifully sung' by Mrs T M Hopkins.[14]

What is omitted from this account is that three motets by Mr E W Elgar were performed on this day: *Domine salvam fac, Salve regina* and *Tantum ergo*. The *Salve Regina*,[15] dated 11 September 1876, an ambitious piece in four sections, is remarkable by reason of its conclusion. Here the choral writing has a sense of continuity in its internal rhythmic progress and a warmth in the harmonic texture, anticipating Elgar's management of choral music in later works:

Ex. 15

Salve Regina

In 1881 the Three Choirs Festival took place in Worcester, and Elgar was promoted to a first violin desk. A year later he was engaged to play in the principal orchestra in Birmingham, conducted by W C Stockley. This acknowledgement of Elgar's skill as violinist brought him into the musical life of Birmingham at a significant point of his career. Until November 1889 he played in every concert in the four-concert annual series.

In the autumn of 1882 a 'Worcestershire Exhibition' took place in the old Engine Works on Shrub Hill. The minutes of a meeting of the organizing committee held at the beginning of June noted that 'offers of organ recitals and other assistance in the musical arrangements had been received from ... Mr E W Elgar'.[16] Disappointed in that application he fared better at the Annual General Meeting of the Amateur Instrumental Society, when he was selected to succeed A J Caldicott – a successful composer of glees – as conductor. At the same time it was important to maintain his standing at St George's, where he succeeded his father as Organist in November 1885. In the same year he must have been gratified by the new organ built for the church by the Belgian firm Anneessens.[17]

On 9 October the new Diocesan bishop – Edward Ilsley – visited St George's for the inauguration of the Apostleship of Prayer and the League of the Sacred Heart. Despite that when he took on the appointment Elgar wrote 'the choir is awful and no good is to be done with them',[18] as usual he obliged the occasion:

. . . some special things had to be sung for which we had no music; then I had to work and compose it all and copy out the parts!! Had to get it in anyhow and broke my neck doing. Anyway the leading paper says the new composition was 'exquisite' so I suppose it was good enough.[19]

The principal work, bringing Elgar's apprenticeship as composer to an end, was *Ecce Sacerdos* magnus, which was to hold a firm place in Catholic worship for some time to come. In 1906 Elgar revised three early works, which were published by Novello as Opus 2 in the next year. An *Ave verum*, originally composed on 28 January 1887 to the text *Pie Jesu*, was in memory of his friend and employer William Allen. The differences between the original and the revision of 1906 are instructive, in marking the distance between apprenticeship and maturity.[20]

Notes

1   Registers of St George's Church, Worcester, (MS) 1685–1778; 1778–1797, continuing; Burial ground Registers 1828–, 1842–, Birmingham Diocesan Archives.
2   BWJ, 18 July.
3   *A Concise History and Description of the City and Cathedral of Worcester*, 3rd edition [1829], p 160.
4   Leicester, H A, *Notes on Catholic Worcester*, Worcester, 1828, p 35.
5   Pio Cianchettini (1790–1851), nephew of J L Dussek and a leading musician in Cheltenham, had a letter from William Leicester of Worcester, asking for the names of possible candidates for the post of organist at St George's. The salary was being raised from £20 to £30 pa (letter from John Bishop, organist of Catholic Church in Cheltenham to his friend Joseph Warren :see pp 36–7).
6   St George's Register.
7   A register of 'Burials in the Parish of St Nicholas Sansome Place at the Catholic Chapel' was followed in 1842 by 'Burials in the Parish of St Nicholas at the Church of the Immaculate Conception in the City of Worcester'. It was not uncommon, in former times, for a chapel to be given one dedication and sometime subsequently to add another. Finally, as at Worcester only the later dedication (of St George) was retained.
8   Robert Berkeley (1794–1874) father of Robert Berkeley (1823–1897).
9   Ernest Newman, *Sunday Times*, 30 October 1955.
10 *Diary of John Evelyn*, ed E S de Beer, Oxford 1955, vol IV of VI, p 345, October 13 1865, Evelyn meeting a Berkeley, who was grandson to the 'honest judge' (Sir Robert Berkeley, d 1656) – see also Trappes-Lomax, T B, 'The Berkeleys of Spetchley and their Contribution to the Survival of the Faith in Worcestershire', Recusant Histories, Biographical Studies 1534–1829, vol I, pp 45–58.
11 'Recollections', by Dr William Done's daughter (Fanny Done) 1921, Worcester Cathedral Library Mus Lib, FA 26.
12 Birthplace Museum, MS 94.
13 BWJ, 5 July 1879.
14 BWJ, 13 June 1880.

15 Birthplace Museum, MS 93.
16 BWJ, 3 June 1882.
17 Organ renovated by Nicholson of Worcester 1890 and 1901, and with additions 1970.
18 Young, *Letters of Edward Elgar*, London 1956, 8 January 1886, p 23.
19 see *Elgar OM*, Percy M Young, London 1955, p 156, fn 1.
20 see *Edward Elgar, Three Motets, Opus 2; a critical edition*, ed Young, Broude Brothers Limited, New York.

8 The Example of St Philip Neri

Part 1

> Palestrina had Father Philip's ministrations in his last moments. Animuccia hung about him during life, sent him a message after death, and was conducted by him through Purgatory to Heaven. And who was he, I say, all the while, but an humble priest?
>
> *The Idea of a University, Discourse IX; 9*

On 1 February 1848 the Oratory was established in Birmingham, its members committed 'to assist the priests at St Chad's [Cathedral]'. A year later the community moved into its first property, a disused gin distillery in Alcester Street. At the end of May F W Faber, with a small group of fellow converts, on Newman's advice left Birmingham for London, where a second Oratory was established. Of this Faber was the first superior. In 1852 the priests of the Birmingham Oratory moved into new buildings in Edgbaston.

The inspiration of St Philip Neri was quickly recognized by Newman's return to poetry. In 1849–50 he wrote some of his most lyrical verses: 'Candlemas', 'The Pilgrim Queen', 'The Month of Mary' and 'The Queen of Seasons (A Song for an inclement May)'. Looking towards Christina Rossetti, these pieces are lightly carried in expectation of later musical setting. In 'The Month of Mary' – each verse is followed by a 'chorus' – the view is out from the streets and alleys of Birmingham:

> Green are the leaves, and sweet the flowers,
>   And rich the hues of May:
> We see them in the gardens round,
>   And market-panniers gay:
> And e'en among our streets, and lanes,
>   And alleys, we descry,
> By fitful gleams, the fair sunshine,
>   The blue transparent sky.

In the same period there were three poems in honour of St Philip Neri, the first opening with this reflection:

> In the far north our lot is cast,
>> Where faithful hearts are few;
> Still are we Philip's children dear,
>> And Peter's soldiers true.

Joseph Gordon, one of the early members of the Oratory, literally merited this description. Born in the West Indies in 1812, he was educated at Rugby School, and then for a time served in the Indian Army. On leaving the Army he went to Cambridge with a view to ordination in the Church of England. Like many others at Cambridge at that time, he was impressed by the forceful preaching of the Evangelical Vicar of Holy Trinity, Charles Simeon. His first curacy, however, was under a well-known Tractarian, W J Irons, theologian and hymn-writer. It was after he had read some of Newman's *Tracts for the Times* that Gordon found an opportunity to go to Oxford, to hear Newman preach. On 20 May 1841 his diary read:

> Ascension. Afterwards we went to St. Mary's to service. Newman read the prayers, and gave a lecture. I was not in the least disappointed in my anticipations, which is saying a great deal. I thought I should have wept from mere fullness of heart. Newman's reading is peculiar and most affecting. His lecture both in style and matter was very like his printed ones and a very good specimen.[1]

Three days later Gordon heard Newman preach again and was no less impressed. However, he continued to serve a further period in the Church of England before he became a Catholic and was ordained into the Oratory community. Endowed with pastoral qualities, being a good manager, effective in dealing with schools, and musical, he worked closely with Newman. He helped in the planning of an Oratory Hymn Book.[2] In spite of being seriously ill – a victim of tuberculosis – in 1851 he was ready to help in the protection of Newman's interests in the notorious lawsuit started against him by a fraudulent Italian priest – Giacinto Achilli.[3] Gordon died on 13 February 1853. How great a shock this was to Newman is revealed by a note, written four years later, on 6 November 1857, at a time of anxiety concerning the function of the Oratory and its future, to Sergeant Edward Bellasis: 'Father Gordon's death was a blow [from] which we shall be long in recovering. It has told in various ways.' The note was never sent.

Faber – noticing how 'Catholics even are said to be sometimes found poring with a devout and unsuspecting delight over the verses of the Olney Hymns' – had published a small collection of hymns in Derby, in 1848.[4] Faber was no musician; Newman was, and in preparing for a complete Hymn Book drew up a detailed outline.[5] In this are his notes on subjects (1–82) to be represented, with textual and thematic incipits. The first page of the outline (nos 1–36) is shown in plate 7. Subsequently, of particular interest nos 42 to 44 are headed 'Guardian Angel', while 'Eternity, Death, Purgatory, Heaven, and Dawn' are numbered from 73 to 78. There are various sketches of music – thematic fragments, melodies, and melodies with elementary harmonizations. In respect of music for general use, Newman was no ascetic. With his experience of teaching music to the children of Littlemore, he was a strong believer in cultivating a popular idiom. In his original music for congregational use Newman shows unexpected facets of personality. So, a robust music-hall idiom introduces the idea of 'Guardian Angels':

Ex. 16

No less inviting was a setting of Faber's 'I was wandering and weary', for 'boys and chorus'. Transposed, and tidied by a more professional musical hand, this appeared, as no 66, in a later Oratory Hymn Book. About the alterations, Newman remarked, 'he had an idea that the words had been somewhat altered to suit his tune'.[6]

Ex. 17

Two simple eight-bar tunes show an engagingly unaffected idiom not dissimilar from that practised by the youthful hymn-composing Elgar of St George's:

Ex. 18

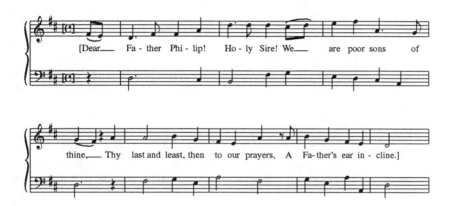

[Dear__ Fa - ther Phi - lip! Ho - ly Sire! We__ are poor sons of

thine,__ Thy last and least, then to our prayers, A Fa- ther's ear in - cline.]

Ex. 19

God of Mer- cy [let us__ run where yon fount of sor- row flows:

Pon- d'ring sweet- ly one by one, Je- su's wounds and Ma- ry's woes.]

Some of the hymns which appeared in the Oratory Hymn Book, being adapted from classical sources, carried a reminder of Newman's chamber music interests. Some came from Reinagle's book.

In 'The Guardian Angel', a poem written in 1853, Newman continued the thought contained in 'Angelic guidance', a poem written at an early point of spiritual crisis.[7] In so doing he released imagery to be taken, in due course, into *The Dream of Gerontius*. The last lines addressed to the angel are:

> Mine, when I stand before the Judge;
> And mine, if spared to stay
> Within the golden furnace, till
> My sin is burn'd away.
>
> And mine, O Brother of my soul
> When my release shall come;
> Thy gentle arms shall lift me then,
> Thy wings shall waft me home.

At this time one of Newman's most earnest young neophytes was Edward Burne-Jones, whose deepest feelings were stirred by the regenerative influence of mediaevalism, the need to save the poor of Birmingham, and the music of Newman's preaching. In Newman's 'The Golden Prison', also of 1853, in the ascent of the pilgrim to 'that golden palace bright', where 'souls elect abide' there is a strain of Pre-Raphaelite sensibility.

In 1850 the Archbishops and Bishops of Ireland, meeting at the National Synod of Thurles, decided to institute a Catholic University of Ireland. A year later, Archbishop Paul Cullen, the principal promoter of the scheme, on behalf of his fellow Bishops, invited Newman to become the first Rector of the proposed University. Although he had many reservations about the wisdom of undertaking such a task when he was otherwise so fully committed, Newman agreed in principle. This happened in the early days of the Oratory, and since he was obliged to concern himself with the complexities of the Achilli affair, his willingness to undertake the direction of the project caused many additional problems. However, despite uncertainty as to the precise nature of his role, he conscientiously undertook the preparation of a series of Inaugural Lectures to be delivered in 1853. These *Discourses*, published under the title *The Idea of a University*, were to become one of Newman's most important works, with lasting influence on educational philosophy.

It was some time before Newman was ready and able to select persons both suitable academically and willing to undertake appointments in the University. There was one young friend in whose abilities he had a particular interest. Henry Scott, born in 1820, from 1838 to 1843 was a Scholar of Trinity College, Oxford, after which, from 1844 to 1850, he was a Fellow of Brasenose. In 1856 he was invited by Newman to join the academic staff of the Catholic University, of which other members were T W Allies, an Oxford convert engaged on a history of Christian civilization, Professor of History and John Hungerford Pollen, Professor of Fine Arts. Pollen, a protégé of Ruskin, was also made responsible for the decoration of the University Church which was opened on 5 June 1856.[8]

Scott, appointed an 'Examiner in Session' of the University – described by Newman as 'not only a good scholar but [one who] has made the sacred text his particular study' – was further suggested as one of a team of translators who were to prepare a new translation of the Bible. Others invited to collaborate in this project were Ambrose St John, Nicholas Darnell, and Edward Caswall, all Fathers of the Oratory. Never enjoying robust health, in the summer of 1859, on medical advice, Scott went with a friend to the Rhineland. His hope was that on his return he would be admitted to the Oratory as a novice.

At the end of August Newman wrote to Scott, adding to his letter, 'Hoping you have by this time parted with your ailment and your doctor'.[9] Although he had been unwell, Scott's death at Kreuznach, near Bingen on 17 September, was unexpected. Newman wrote to William Sullivan a month later, 'Alas, poor Scott is no more . . . It has been a great grief to us'. With this letter he enclosed an unfinished essay by Scott on the Picturesque, 'a subject on which hardly two people will agree together.' By his Will, made at Nice in 1856, Scott left all his books, which are now in the Oratory Library, to Newman. These included *The Pilgrim's Progress*, with Southey's 'Life of Bunyan' and an introductory poem by Cowper (1830), and *In Memoriam* (1850), Tennyson's tribute to Arthur Hallam, his friend who died in youth.

Sometime during his days as a student at Oxford – possibly in 1819 – Newman had a strange premonition, which was written into a notebook:

> Make a poem on Faith. Bring in the plague of Athens as one of the examples; a maid dying over her cursing and blaspheming lover. The eastern Philosopher. To end with a faint imagination of the soul just freed from the bonds of the mortal body.[10]

Newman's *Dream of Gerontius*, published a year after the *Apologia*, unlike *In Memoriam*, was written in one night. On 16 June 1865, to John Telford, who suggested, 'I should like to have seen our Dear Blessed Lady appear', Newman wrote:

> I have said what I saw . . . I have set down the dream as it came before the dreamer. It is not my fault if the sleeper did not dream any more. Perhaps something awoke him. Dreams are generally fragmentary. I have nothing more to tell.[11]

On 11 October he wrote to Allies, 'On the 17th of January last it came into my head to write it, I really cannot tell how. And I wrote on till it was finished . . .'.[12] A somewhat similar process is explained elsewhere in a note left by a writer of a different order – the late John Buchan: 'I never consciously invented with a pen in my hand; I waited until the story had told itself and then wrote it down, and since it was already a finished thing, I wrote it fast.[13]

While *The Dream of Gerontius* was a memorial to Joseph Gordon, it also enshrined Newman's intimate memories of others: of his father who died soon after his ordination in 1824, of his youngest sister Mary in 1828, of his mother in the spring of 1836, shortly after the death of Froude. In that dreams are to be thought of as reflections of past experience, *The Dream of Gerontius* is a continuum of past experience seeking expression.

As there are frequent indications of the pattern of *Gerontius* in the poems, so too in some of the sermons preached in Oxford. Concerning 'the gift of sleep', God 'afflicts us', but 'breaks our trial into portions', and 'takes us out of this world ever and anon, and gives us a holyday-time, like children at school, in an unknown and mysterious country'.[14]

In a Lenten sermon, 'The Individuality of the Soul', he says:

> The point to be considered is this, that every soul of man which is or has been on earth, has a separate existence; and that, in eternity, not in time merely . . . . Nothing is more difficult than to realize that every man has a distinct soul.[15]

In the same sermon, in an unconscious reference to Bunyan's 'Vanity Fair', Newman looks at 'the populous town . . . crowds in streets . . . full shops . . . [and] houses full of people', which gives;

> a general idea of splendour, magnificence, opulence, and energy. But what is the truth? Why, that every being in that great concourse is his own centre, and all this about him are but shades, but a 'vain shadow', in which he 'walketh and disquieteth himself in vain'. He has his own hopes and fears, desires, judgments, and aims; he is everything, and no one else is really anything. No one outside of him can really touch him, can touch his soul, his immortality; he must live within himself for ever. He has a depth within him unfathomable, an infinite abyss of existence; and the scene in which he becomes part for the moment is but a gleam of sunshine upon its surface.

Directly to the point of departure of the poem to come is this majestic passage in a New Year sermon:

> But let us follow the course of a soul thus casting off the world, and cast off by it. It goes forth as a stranger on a journey. Man seems to die and to be no more, when he is but quitting us, and is really beginning to live. Then he sees sights which before it did not even enter into his mind to conceive, and the world is even less to him than he to the world. Just now he was lying on the bed of sickness, but in that moment of death what an awful change has come over him! What a crisis before him! There is a stillness in the room that lately held him; nothing is doing there, for he is gone, he now belongs to others; he now belongs entirely to the Lord who brought him; to Him he returns; but whether to be lodged safely in His place of hope, or to be imprisoned against the great Day, that is another matter, that depends on the deeds done in the body, whether good or evil.[16]

In the Whitsuntide sermon of 1841, there is a further reflection of

Bunyan's report given to Christian by two men who had seen the hobgoblins, satyrs and dragons and heard the continual howling and yelling of the underworld:

> Again, the sight of an assemblage of beasts of prey and other ferocious animals, their strangeness and startling novelty, the originality (if I may use the term) and mysteriousness of their forms, and gestures, and habits, and their variety and independence of one another, expand the mind, not without its own consciousness; as if knowledge were a real opening, and as if an addition to the external objects presented before it were an addition to its inward powers.[17]

For the Feast of the Purification in 1843 Newman remembers Isaac Williams and the compelling thought of a 'perpetual choir':

> In the capitals of Christendom the high cathedral and the perpetual choir still witness to the victory of Faith over the world's power. To see its triumph over the world's wisdom, we must enter those solemn cemeteries in which are stored the relics and the monuments of ancient Faith – our libraries. Look along their shelves, and every name you read there is, in one sense or other, a trophy set up in record of the victories of Faith.[18]

The first draft of *The Dream of Gerontius* was contained in 52 scraps of paper. A fair copy, begun on 17 January, was completed by 7 February 1865 (a week before the death of Cardinal Wiseman). On All Souls Day, 2 November 1865, Newman wrote to Father Philip Gordon, of the London Oratory, 'I was prompted to it by that never sleeping remembrance which I have of your dear Brother'. In this fair copy the Hymn for the Dead, 'Help, Lord' (in 1857, published in Newman's *Verses on Various Occasions*, p 306), was inserted after Psalm XC, for the Souls in Purgatory. Of the psalm this was an original translation – neither based on Douai nor the Authorized Version. A copy of the whole work was sent to Father H J Coleridge, editor of *The Month II*, where it was published in two parts, in the May and June issues. It was separately published in London in the same year by Burns and Oates. Translations of *The Dream of Gerontius* were published in France in 1869 and 1889, and in Germany in 1885. By the time of Newman's death the 27th edition had appeared in England.

During the nineteenth century and at least through Edwardian times the pattern of general life was designed to accommodate the imagery of death. As were Newman's and Elgar's experiences, death came into families with a degree of awful familiarity. Outside the house traffic in the street would be dampened by bark laid over the cobbles; the church bell tolled. The funeral ritual was full, and awful. Funeral orations, in the simplest settings, contained consoling imagery not imaginable in modern times. *The Dream of Gerontius* was in its time intelligible – as now, in general, it cannot be, unless with the timeless aid of music.

Part 2

The proper aim of the Oratory in Birmingham, according to the Papal brief which was its charter, was 'the cultivation of a superior Catholic educated class'. In 1856, aware of all the difficulties to be encountered, Newman noted how permisssion had been received from Rome to set up two schools 'congenial to the spirit of St Philip': a school of painting, and a school of music.

> These arts are naturally congenial to young minds, and in Birmingham especially. Music is one of the special characteristics of the Oratory, and it is the art for which Birmingham is famous. A school of painting, on the other hand, is a great *desideratum* in England; we have about us various youths who have a talent in that line, and there are various arts in Birmingham, which would naturally group themselves under a school of ecclesiastical painting and decoration.[19]

If the hope to establish a school of painting went no further than to give encouragement to the young Edward Burne-Jones, it was otherwise with music, for Newman was supported by a sequence of musical colleagues. The first Prefect of Music was Father Bowles, a cellist who had taken part in occasional chamber music performance at Oscott. Newman succeeded Bowles as Prefect of Music before giving the place to Ambrose St John, who was for some years Newman's secretary. A choir, sometimes of boys, sometimes of men, and finally of mixed voices, was developed and on 19 August 1877, an organ was installed. This, the gift of Richard Bellasis, sometime Prefect of Music, inspired the engagement of a professional organist. The first, Egerton Hardy, moved to Ushaw in 1884 and was succeeded by William Sewell, who remained in office, exercising influence not only in the Oratory but in Catholic music generally, for more than twenty years.

Of those who served as Prefects of Music, the most significant contributions were made by Richard Bellasis,[20] Anthony Pollen, William Neville and Robert Eaton, to whom Sewell dedicated an expressive Mass in A flat. Bellasis, whose youngest brother, Henry was also an Oratorian, was a son of Edward Bellasis, Sergeant-at-Law, an Oxford friend of Newman who became a Catholic in 1850. Before becoming an Oratorian, Pollen, a son of John Hungerford Pollen, had served as a sailor. At various times the Prefects of Music, as well as Newman himself, taught in the Oratory School founded in 1859. As he had done long before in Littlemore, Newman took a personal interest in the musical activities of pupils. From time to time he played the violin at school concerts and often was present at chamber music practices.[21]

The most influential practical musician in Birmingham at that time was W C Stockley, who – active for fifty years – was chorus-master for the

Triennial Festivals, and conductor of regular seasonal series of orchestral concerts in the Town Hall. Newman took great pleasure in going to concerts and could be eloquent in critical comment. Nor was he hesitant in showing his acquaintance with the technicalities of musical structure.

In 1867 he heard *Elijah*, conducted by Michael Costa at the opening concert of the Birmingham Festival. This performance he recollected four years later, when on a snowy night in March 1871 he went to a concert at the Town Hall with William Neville. He wrote to Edward Bellasis:

> Every beginner deals in diminished sevenths. At least it was as a boy I first discovered the chord from the Overture to Zauberflöte; and henceforth it figured with powerful effect in my compositions. You must try to make a melody. Without it you cannot compose. Perhaps, however, it is that which makes a musical genius. I was very much disappointed at the one time that I heard the Elijah, not to meet with a beautiful melody from beginning to end. What can be more beautiful . . . than Handel's, Mozart's, and Beethoven's melodies?[22]

In 1876 he went to the last day of the Birmingham Music Festival (1 September) with Bellasis and Arthur [Pollen], hearing, in the morning, Spohr's *Last Judgement*, Wagner's *Love Feast of the Apostles*, Beethoven's Mass in C and, in the evening, Mendelssohn's *St Paul*.

Three years later Newman wrote to Stockley, thanking him for obtaining tickets for the Festival concerts on 27 and 29 August:

> My companions join me in thanking you for the great civility you have shown to us and the trouble you have taken in getting us seats in the Town Hall on Wednesday and today. It was not thrown away, for we received high gratification from the magnificent compositions of the great masters who were selected for the concerts on those two dates.[23]

On Wednesday 27 August the principal work was Rossini's *Moses in Egypt*; on Friday the morning concert comprised Cherubini's Requiem in C minor and Schubert's *Salve Regina* (Op 47), while *Israel in Egypt* was given in the evening. Newman was particularly impressed by Cherubini.

In instrumental music he was faithful to the classics, above all to Mozart and Beethoven. At one Festival concert in 1882, a lady who came in late 'chattered away behind us like a magpie' during the performance of Mozart's G minor Symphony, a work of 'exuberant inventiveness' he once said, which was as dear to Newman's as to Elgar's heart.[24] At the end of the day, however, it was Beethoven who stood first in his respect. In a powerful passage in *The Idea of a University* he considers Beethoven (without naming him) at great length – and the relationship with religion of music itself:

> Rising in his strength he will break through the trammels of words; he will scatter human voices, even the sweetest, to the winds; he will be borne upon nothing less than the fullest flood of sounds which art has enabled him to

draw from mechanical contrivances; he will go forth as a giant, as far as ever his instruments can reach, starting from their secret depths fresh and fresh elements of beauty and grandeur as he goes, and putting them together into still more marvellous and rapturous combinations.[25]

Stockley was well-known to the Oratory. For example, he selected the singers for a performance of Cherubini's Requiem in D minor for male voices, which he conducted on 13 November 1885. Cardinal Newman was present at the concert, which was in memory of former pupils of the Oratory School.

In 1881 this same work had been included in a Three Choirs Festival programme at Worcester on the suggestion of W H Elgar, whose son Edward in that year was promoted to playing first violin in the Festival Orchestra. From 1882, for six years, he also played in Stockley's orchestra, 'a really first-class band . . . of 80 skilled players . . .' which, with a few picked London professionals, achieved 'a unity, precision, and perfect balance of parts which any Metropolitan organisation might envy.'[26]

It was on the suggestion of George Hope Johnstone — with the promise of financial support should it be needed — that the orchestra was built up to its full strength. The concerts were maintained for twenty-four years, and Stockley (himself a self-educated musician) was consistently eager to assist young composers. Not all of them achieved distinction. Orchestral pieces of Elgar were included in his programmes in 1883 (*Intermezzo moresque*), 1885 (*Sevillana* – 'by a member of Mr Stockley's orchestra'), and on 23 February, 1888 (*Three Pieces for Small orchestra*).

It was at the Three Choirs Festival of 1884 that Elgar, as violinist, became aware of the music of Dvořák, in particular the *Stabat Mater* and the Symphony in D. In an unaccustomed spirit of tolerance – not to be maintained by some of their successors – the Dean and Chapter of Worcester raised no objection to the performance of a Catholic work with a Latin text. Of the symphony, Elgar wrote to his friend Dr Charles Buck, 'It is simply ravishing, so tuneful and clever and the orchestration is wonderful: no matter how few instruments he uses it never sounds thin'.[27] Elgar was to have another opportunity of studying the symphony from the inside in 1886, when playing in Stockley's orchestra. At this Festival Elgar took part in the performance of another relatively new work: Gounod's *The Redemption*, which had been commissioned for the Birmingham Festival of 1882, and was given in Three Choirs Festivals at Worcester in 1884 and Hereford in 1885. The Hereford programme also included Dvořák's *Stabat Mater*, which was heard again at Gloucester in 1886.

Gounod disposed his talents with equal success in opera and oratorio. A profoundly religious person, sometime seminary student, he counted himself a disciple of Palestrina, and in later life devoted himself to sacred music. His major work, *The Redemption*, is a trilogy in which the first part concerns Christ's Passion and Death, the second, from the Resurrection to the Ascension, and the third, Pentecost and the spread of Christianity. In the Preface Gounod selfconsciously drew attention to his two dominant motifs – the first representing 'Atonement', the second being the plainsong hymn *Vexilla Regis prodeunt*. At the final rehearsal of this work Newman was among a privileged audience.

For the Birmingham Festival of 1885 – Hans Richter succeeding Costa as conductor – Gounod offered *Mors et Vita*, the text in Latin. After a prologue the three movements denote *Mors*, *Judicium*, and *Vita*. Gounod introduced the work thus:

> It will perhaps be asked why, in the title, I have placed death before life, although in the order of temporal things life precedes death. Death is only the end of that existence which dies each day; it is only the end of a continual 'dying'. But it is the first moment, and, as it were, the birth of that which dies no more.

Although Handel and Mendelssohn had by no means been jettisoned by the Birmingham Committee, there was a distinct shift of mood away from the familiar oratorios and casual cantatas towards works distinguished by a late romantic high seriousness. Hence the shock administered by Dvořák's offer of *The Spectre's Bride* (Op 69) for the Festival of 1885. The success of his *Stabat Mater* had led the Committee to suppose that he would offer a 'sacred' work. When first proposed, *The Spectre's Bride* immediately impressed itself by its unsuitability:

> As we have already mentioned, the work chosen by a composer for a Festival may not be of the same character as those by which he has made a name in this country; and when, therefore, Dvořák decided to write a secular Cantata a certain amount of anxiety might reasonably be felt by the Committee to be the result.[28]

During his visit to Birmingham to conduct the first performance of *The Spectre's Bride* it is not impossible that Dvořák visited the Oratory. There is, however, no evidence that he did so. That he was at some time presented with a copy of *Gerontius* in the German edition is not in doubt. When and who the donor was is not known. A rumour long persisted that at the time of his Birmingham visit in 1885, Dvořák was invited to compose a setting of *The Dream* for the 1888 Birmingham Festival.

Three composers – one of them was Dvořák – had turned down opportunities to offer works for the Festival of that year.[29] There was no suggestion that in Dvořák's case it was to have been a setting of any part of *The Dream of Gerontius*, nor among his surviving sketches was there ever found material supporting such a claim.[30] For a Birmingham Festival commission for 1891 Dvořák composed the Requiem, which one Czech scholar — Jarmil Burghauser — believes to have been inspired by Newman's poem. The only support to this hypothesis is a letter written to Novello (publisher of the work) on 28 August 1891: 'I wish no dedication on the title page of the vocal score or full score'. Perhaps a Dedication to Newman may have been at first intended.

Misinformation concerning Dvořák's supposed connection with *The Dream* grew progressively and romantically. On 24 March 1900 the *Lady's Pictorial*, referring to Elgar's forthcoming *Dream of St Gerontius* [*sic*], wrote of 'a poem that Dvořák was attracted by some years ago, though the Bohemian Composer subsequently abandoned the idea of setting it'. In 1939 W H Reed supposed that, after the composer had attended High Mass at the Oratory,'the cardinal presented him with a copy of *Gerontius* [and that]

> Dvořák left in high glee, saying that it would inspire him. It was indeed suggested to the festival committee that he should be invited to write a setting for the 1888 Birmingham Festival.

Reed claimed to have had an account of 'the first performance' [of *Gerontius*] 'written by the Rev Robert Eaton'.[31] In view of the fact that Eaton wrote elsewhere concerning *Gerontius*, it seems that Reed's memory was playing him false. Later writers have copied Reed, in some cases further embellishing his account.

In the event Newman, who had been created cardinal in the previous year, became involved in the 1888 Festival at a very early stage, at which point it would not have been possible for him not to have been aware of any proposed setting of *Gerontius*. On 27 December 1886 he wrote to Father William Philip Gordon — brother of Joseph Gordon — a Father of the London Oratory, asking if he might be able to persuade the Duke of Norfolk to be President of the next (the thirty-sixth) Birmingham Music Festival. To the Duke — a former pupil of the Oratory school — he also wrote personally. If the Duke would be able to accept an invitation to act as President of the Birmingham Music Festival in 1888 it would not only be generally appreciated, but it would also

> . . . continue and increase the good will already felt towards us by the local musical world, which is a special power in Birmingham, and with which through our two Fathers Bellasis we are on excellent terms.
>   There is another consideration which occurs to me, it is this — though politics and religion are prohibited and impossible in a musical undertaking, it is impossible too, that the sight of your Grace should fail to inspire friendly thoughts both towards yourself and towards Catholics, a consideration not to be overlooked in a place and time in which lately there has been so much modification of opinion . . . .[32]

Newman became a vice president of the festival of 1888, having his place on the programme immediately below the last Duke (of Portland) on the list. The Bishop of Worcester and the Deans of Worcester and Lichfield were also vice presidents. To each of the morning concerts the president, the Duke of Norfolk, was accompanied by the cardinal.

The principal works at the Festival were, on 28 August: *Elijah*, Dvořák's *Stabat Mater*, and the 'Jupiter' Symphony; 29 August: Parry's *Judith* and Sullivan's *Golden Legend*; 30 August: *Messiah* and Frederick Bridge's *Callirhoë* ('New Cantata'); 31 August: Bach, *Magnificat*, Beethoven, Fifth Symphony, Berlioz, *Messe des Morts*: and Handel, *Saul*.

The programme book included an analysis of Dvořák's *Stabat Mater* by Joseph Bennett, which, with a suitable undertone of critical caution, ended:

> To sum up – this 'Stabat Mater' is a notable work, and approaches as near to greatness as possible, if it be not actually destined to rank among world-renowned masterpieces. It is fresh and new, while in harmony with the established canon of art; and, though apparently laboured and over-developed in places, speaks with the force and directness of genius.

By this time the repertory of the Oratory choir had become extensive, drawing music-lovers from across the neighbourhood. A representative programme, with orchestra, given in the Exchange Room in Birmingham on 11 July 1890, included parts of Masses and Motets by Beethoven, Cherubini, Costa, Robert Führer (Organist of the Cathedral in Prague), Gounod, Hummel, Niedermeyer, and Reissiger. An *Ave Maria* by William Sewell, the Oratory organist, was also sung. The conductor was Richard Bellasis. Sunday music at the Oratory similarly covered a wide range.

There is one notable connection between the Oratory and Dvořák which was recorded in the Oratory Choir Book of 1893, by Father Robert Eaton. On Rosary Sunday, 1 October 1893, at the Oratory, Dvořák's Mass in D was performed; 'probably', according to the *Daily Mail* and *Daily Post* of 2 October, 'the first performance in England in connection with its ecclesiastical purport' . . . . If there was any occasion which should have stimulated discussion of Dvořák visiting the Oratory at any time, or memories of any interest in the possibility of his setting *The Dream of Gerontius* this – with the newspapers alerted – was it.

While Dvořák cannot be shown to have pursued the idea of setting *The Dream of Gerontius* to music, there were others who entertained ambitions in that direction. In the early 1870s Frederick Bridge, recently appointed Organist of Manchester Cathedral, in search of a text from which to make a choral and orchestral work for submission for an Oxford Mus D degree, was urged by an old friend – a Catholic priest now living in Worcestershire – to consider *The Dream*.[33] With a generous acknowledgement of his own limitations Bridge conceded, 'the subject seemed beyond my powers'. In its place he successfully submitted an oratorio, *Mount Moriah*.

At the Hereford Festival of 1891 a motet, 'Praise to the holiest in the height' was included as 'one of the novelties of the Festival' The composer, Dr Henry John Edwards, was the Organist of Barnstaple parish church. The inclusion of this work in the Hereford programme displeased another composer: the Reverend Samuel James Rowton, MA of Durham, and Mus D both of Nürnberg and Dublin, composer of hymns and songs for Epsom College, of which he was choirmaster. He wrote as follows to Father William Neville:

The College, Epsom.

Sept 14 [1891]

Dear Sir

   May I recall to your memory the correspondence we had a year ago on the subject of some music of mine, to words from the Dream of Gerontius? – I observe from the public papers that a performance was given just lately at the Festival of the Three Choirs, of music by another composer to words from the same work – words some of which were included in my request to you. Kindly inform me if this was done with your knowledge and consent.

   I am credibly advised that there is now no longer any legal restriction on the words of the Dream, which came out in 1865, and some portions of which have appeared in well known Hymnals of the Church of England.

I am, dear sir, yours faithfully,

   S. J. Rowton.[34]

The previous letter does not seem to exist, nor is it known how Neville replied.

   In 1892 Edward Bellasis's 'Cardinal Newman as a Musician' first published in *The Month*, September 1891, was reprinted by Kegan Paul. A note on p 3, not in the 1891 version, was added: 'Rev S J Rouston [*sic*] has musically essayed the Dream of Gerontius.' Rowton's ambitions did not generally extend beyond school songs (to Latin texts) and hymn tunes.

   Four years later Edmund Horace Fellowes, BA fittingly of Oriel College, and now a curate in London, successfully submitted the Hymn of the / Third choir of Angelicals / from the Dream of Gerontius / set to music / for/ Soprano solo, quartett, chorus and / string orchestra for the Mus.B degree in 1895.[35]

   The work consists of four sections: Chorus, 'Praise to the holiest';

Soprano solo, 'The angels, as beseechingly'; Quartett, 'But to the younger race', Chorus, 'Praise to the holiest'.

Ex. 20

Ex. 21

So far as is known that was the end of Fellowes's career as composer. His exercise was, however, the prelude to a distinguished career, in the course of which he made familiar many masterpieces by English composers of the sixteenth and seventeenth centuries.

Notes

1   Tristram, *Newman and his Friends*, p 108 f.
2   *Collection of Hymns in Use at the Oratory of St Philip Neri at Birmingham*, Birmingham/London, Powell & Co, 1856.
3   Giacinto Achilli, a renegade monk, began an action for libel against Newman, who had publicly denounced him as being an immoral person. In 1852 a jury, which had heard the case, determined that it was not proved, as a result of which Newman incurred heavy costs (defrayed through public subscription). Edward Bellasis acted for Newman.
4   'It was natural that an English son of St Philip, should feel the want of a collection of English Catholic hymns fitted for singing ... the Author's ignorance of music appeared in some measure to disqualify him for the work of supplying the defect .... The MS of the present volume was submitted to a musical friend, who replied that certain verses of all or nearly all the hymns would do for singing: and this encouragement has led to its publication.' (*Preface*), 1849.
5   Oratory MS A5.2.
6   Bellasis, E, 'Cardinal Newman as a Musician', *The Month*, LXXIII, September 1891, p 1 f.
7   See *Apologia* I, p 76.
8   In 1844 Pollen, who was on the fringe of the Pre-Raphaelite movement, painted the ceiling of Merton College, Oxford. Ordained in the Church of England, he was converted to Rome in 1852. Gerard Manley Hopkins, writing to Newman from Dublin on 20 February 1884 mentioned the dowdy look of the former university buildings, '. . . only one looks bright, and that no longer belongs to the college, the little church of of your building, the Byzantine style of which reminds me of the Oratory and bears your impress clearly enough'.
9   LD XIII, p 294.
10 *John Henry Newman, Autobiographical Writings, Casual Thoughts set down as they occurred, 1817–26*, ed H Tristram, London, 1937.
11 LD XXI, p 498.
12 LD XXII, p 72.
13 John Buchan, note in John Buchan Museum, Broughton, Lanark.
14 *Selections from Parochial and Plain Sermons, Selections adapted to the Seasons*, 1878; 'Present Blessings', Septuagesima, p 108.
15 Ibid, 'The Individuality of the Soul', p 132.
16 *Parochial and Plain Sermons*, Selection, 1878, New Year Sermon, 'The 'Lapse of Time', p 47.
17 *Parochial and Plain Sermons*, vol III, 'Wisdom contrasted with Faith and with Bigotry', p 283.
18 *Parochial and Plain Sermons*, vol III, 1878, Feast of the Purification, 'The Theory of Developments in Religious Doctrine', p 315.
19 'Remarks on the Oratorian Vocation', *Newman's Oratory Papers*, nos 24 & 25, p 309, rough draft.
20 Richard Garnett Bellasis, pupil in Oratory School at the time of its opening in May 1859, stayed until 1870. He began to study law, but joined the Oratory in 1875 and was ordained in 1879; founder and first principal of St. Phillip's Grammar School; Superior of Oratory 1911–23. Sergeant Edward Bellasis ((1800–1873), educated Christ's Hospital and Oxford, became barrister

engaged particularly in Parliamentary business, leaving his influence on several Acts. Dedicatee of *The Grammar of Assent*.

21 Elwes, Winifride and Richard, *Gervase Elwes: the Story of his Life*, London, 1935, p 30.

22 LD xxv (2 March) 1871, p 295; in respect of Festival performance of *Elijah* on 1 October 1867, Henry Lunn described 'a gigantic orchestra, filled with the best instrumentalists in Europe, [and] the most properly trained choristers ever assembled within a building . . . the sublimity of the choruses with which this work abounds has never been so conspicuously brought out as on this occasion' (*Mus T*, p 165).

23 LD xxix, p 174, 27 & 29 August.

24 Bellasis, op cit, p 11.

25 *Idea of a University*, dis 1v, 80, 81.

26 *Mus T*, xxvi,1885, p 597.

27 Young, *Elgar OM*, p 56.

28 *Mus T* xxvi, Sept 1885, p 530.

29 'There is no law by which a composer can be forced to carry out a promise against which he pleads lack of opportunity or health; otherwise we should have seen the names of Dvořák, Mackenzie, and Goring Thomas in the list.' *Mus T*, xxix, 1888, p 600.

30 I am obliged to Dr Jan Smaczny for relevant information from Czech sources concerning Dvořák and Newman.

31 Reed, W H, *Elgar*, 1939, p 59. See R Eaton in Chapter 12, concerning Worcester performance of *Gerontius* (1902).

32 LD xxxi, p 181, 1977.

33 Bridge, Frederick, *A Westminster Pilgrim*, London 1918, p 60.

34 Letter in Oratory archives.

35 Oxford, Bodleian Library, MS Mus Sch, Ex d 224.

9 '... A Triumph of Faith'

On 8 May 1889 Edward Elgar and Alice Roberts were married in the spendid new church – completed only in 1884 – of Brompton Oratory. The officiating priest was Father Alfred Fawkes.[1] A month after their wedding, on Whitsunday, 9 June, the Elgars went to the Pro-Cathedral in Kensington to hear a sermon by Cardinal Manning – then at the height of his fame. It was, however, the music that captured Elgar's attention. He was not enchanted with the performance of the choir: Haydn's second Mass, he said, was 'awful'. This was the prelude to mounting disenchantment.

Progress on the way to becoming a composer was painfully slow, for a modest reputation gained in the provinces counted for little in London. However, it was not quite easy to leave the provinces behind and on 7 November he was back on familiar ground. It was worth going to Birmingham to play for Stockley – for the last time, as he thought. It was, as usual, a too full programme of works, great and small, by Meyerbeer, Gounod, Mackenzie, Parry, Weber, Sullivan, Tito Battei, Beethoven, and Frederick Cliffe. Here was Elgar coming up from London to play in a Symphony in C minor (no 1), by another provincial composer. What is more, having been born in Bradford in 1857 Cliffe was Elgar's exact contemporary. Clearly he was a composer of the moment, for his symphony had already enjoyed two Crystal Palace performances earlier in the year.[2] The Leeds Festival, having rejected this work for the Festival of 1889, quickly commissioned Cliffe's second Symphony for the next Leeds Festival.

In August 1890 a daughter, Carice, had been born and – from the tone of his letter of August 21 to his sister Helen – it is clear that Worcester was much in Elgar's mind: 'Are you', he asked, thinking of the forthcoming Three Choirs Festival, 'going to do anything special at Church for the edification of the visitors?'

Next month Elgar went back to Worcester to take his place once more in the Festival orchestra, from which he was called to conduct the first performance of his *Froissart* overture. That this was included in the programme was due to Done – now at the very end of his half-century of service to the cathedral and the Festival. The principal new English work that year was by Frederick Bridge (whose thoughts had once turned to the subject of *Gerontius*). His oratorio, *The Repentance of Nineveh* went well, except that the supplementary 'invisible choir' – singing consistently flat – was too distinctly audible. In Beethoven's *Engedi* (or *Mount of Olives*) the conductor was at one point required 'to beat the actual desk as well as the metaphorical time'. Such was then the standard of performance at the Three Choirs Festival.

Elgar, who conducted his own work, received not much more than half-hearted commendation in the October issue of *The Musical Times*: 'Froissart was much applauded – the prophet had honour even in his own country'. It was ten years before *Froissart* was heard in London, and then it was conducted by Heinrich Sück, who was to take over Elgar's Worcester violin-teaching practice. One other new name appeared on the Worcester programme, that of Harry Plunket Greene, who had spent some years studying in Stuttgart and – in the previous year – had impressed Cosima Wagner. On Sunday, after the Festival had ended, Elgar attended mass at St George's, went to the cathedral for matins, and in the evening resumed his old seat to play the organ for benediction.

After his small success with *Froissart* at the Festival, there was little to be enthusiastic about from the reactions of the various publishers Elgar visited. The weather at the turn of the year was particularly depressing. 30 December Alice thought 'the coldest day she had ever felt (I cried with the cold)'. Edward was preparing letters to influential acquaintances to request their availability as references. It was a very difficult winter, and London in every way inhospitable. Writing to his Worcester friend, Frank Webb, on 8 February, he accurately described a 'London fog' as 'a sort of yellow darkness. I grasped my way to church this morning & returned in an hour's time a weird & blackened thing with a great & giddy headache'.

Three days later Elgar was again in Birmingham, where Stockley, consistently loyal to him, included *Froissart* in his programme. Something recognizable as the spirit of Elgarianism was caught in the programme note: '. . . a powerful *coda* brings the orchestra discourse about love, romance, and martial prowess to an impressive conclusion'. Alice's note was, 'E. called & applauded on to platform. A. very proud'. That was but one event which helped to relieve a depressing period throughout which Elgar's hypochondriacal tendencies asserted themselves. For a time he complained regularly of trouble with his eyes (it was never established what the trouble was). Having suffered a painful wisdom tooth at the end of 1890, an infection of the tonsils caused a severe sore throat.

By June depression was complete. The Elgars gave up in London and returned to Worcestershire. Edward knew that here he could at least earn a living. On 20 June they spent their first night in the Malvern house – 'Forli' – which was to be their home for the next few years. Back to the routine of provincial music-making and of teaching the violin to unwilling school-girls, Elgar relied on the confidence placed in him by his friends. By the summer of 1892 the *Serenade for Strings* and the cantata *The Black Knight* were reasonably advanced. In August he and Alice were able to holiday in Bavaria, where they were brought into the familiarities of Catholic worship in a Bavarian peasant culture. On 8 August Elgar wrote to his Grafton nephews and nieces[3] a charming account of the devotions of the country people in Oberstdorf, and of the church music:

> Now this is so different to England because it is a Catholic country & in this part there are no protestants: & the church is open all day & you see workmen & workwomen carrying their rosaries & they go into the church as they pass by & say a few prayers (like you do without going to church) & then they come out of church & go on with their work. & then during mass at the elevation they ring one of the great bells in the church tower & all the people in the street know it is the elevation & take off their hats & make the sign of the Cross! On the roads here there are crucifixes very often & generally a few trees planted round them for shade & people passing by say a prayer & rest and then go on their way. The music in Church is nice but very odd to us. They have a violin & a hautboy & a clarinet & a trombone which made such a noise.[4]

Hubert Leicester, who was choirmaster at St George's, had asked that Edward – while in Germany – might look out for any music that could be useful for his choir. In his response Edward mentioned 'a good Mass done by the villagers, very well conducted by the schoolmaster with whom I subsequently became acquent: he let me look over their stock & I made notes thereon'. This mass, by a local composer, in manuscript parts, was not going to be useful to Leicester. However, Elgar made a note of other possibilities – 'no display & no flourishes, but plain, nicely harmonised music'.[5] In the following year the Elgars were again in Germany and were able to visit Oberammergau where Edward attended the opening of an organ and also played it.[6]

In April 1893 Elgar's first cantata-style work, *The Black Knight*, for chorus and orchestra, was performed by the Worcester Festival Choral Society. Composed within the conventions of a choral society romantic narrative, there is in *The Black Knight* a freedom from the narrow compositional manners of the day: in compelling rhythm, spacious choral display, and exploitation of tonal ambiguities. Not inappropriately it is a work with a German accent.

As the Three Choirs Festival took place in Worcester again in 1893, Elgar registered his continuing disappointment: 'I played 1st violin for the sake of the fee as I c^d obtain no recognition as a composer'.[7] The principal new work was Parry's *Job*, in which Plunket Greene was the principal soloist.

Although Elgar was continually dissatisfied by his slow progress, he was becoming known among the Catholic communities of the Midlands. On 27 October 1893 a new altar was consecrated by Bishop Ilsley in the enlarged chancel of St Catherine's Church in Birmingham. The orchestra was led on this occasion by Herr Sück. The introit was Elgar's *Ecce sacerdos magnus*.[8] A month later the new church of St Osburg in Coventry was opened in the presence of Cardinal Herbert Vaughan, who had succeeded Manning as Archbishop of Westminster in the previous year.

> Elgar's 'Ecce Sacerdos', which heralded the approach into the church of the Cardinal's procession, is a beautifully written piece, and fits the subject as well as it could be done.[9]

This notice suggested that Elgar had orchestrated the work for this particular occasion (which was probably not the case), and added 'that it was much admired by the Cardinal'.

Soon Elgar's reputation as composer was seen to be moving out of the narrow confines of Midland approval. At the meeting of the Guarantors of the North Staffordshire Musical Festival, held on 17 December 1895, it was reported that 'Mr. Edward Elgar, of Malvern, had been approached by Dr. Swinnerton Heap [also chorus master of the Birmingham Triennial Festival], and had agreed to produce a new work at the Festival to be held in October 1896'.[10] The Organ Sonata and the evocative *Songs from the Bavarian Highlands* were published in 1896, and *Lux Christi* was performed at the Three Choirs Festival in Worcester. On 9 November the first performance of *King Olaf* took place at the North Staffordshire Festival in Hanley. Elgar, who had played in the orchestra for the Festival of 1888, conducted the performance and also that of *Sevillana* at the Cheltenham Festival that followed. Next he went to Hereford, to talk to Sinclair about the *Te Deum and Benedictus* commissioned for the next Three Choirs Festival. At home, at least, Elgar was in danger of becoming famous. Ending a sequence of notices of *King Olaf* and *Sevillana*, a local newspaper remarked:

> There was bye-the-bye, a splendid appropriateness in the Benediction Service at St. George's Catholic Church on Sunday night, when the Litany of the Virgin was sung to a very melodious and effective setting by Mr. Edward

Elgar, who some years ago was organist at this church and whose choir music he had enriched with many excellent little compositions.[11]

The performance of the *Te Deum and Benedictus* at the Hereford Festival of 1897 found *The Musician* somewhat confused by Elgar's style, in which there appeared traces of both Verdi and Brahms. Clearly there was a new and distinctive tone in the area of church music. What infuriated the critic, however, was what must also have concerned Elgar.

> But what can be expected with such very limited opportunities of rehearsal? In England we make a virtue of necessity, and, because of the difficulty and expense of getting a competent orchestra together, have to cultivate the art of slipping through difficult places as easily as may be.[12]

As the first phase of Elgar's career ended, and in anticipation of the first performance of *Caractacus* to take place at the Leeds Festival on 5 October 1898, a glance into the future was taken by the *Yorkshire Post*:

> ... Elgar in his teens as deputy to his father, and later succeeding him in the organ gallery, at once plunging into composition, producing motets, masses, and every kind of church music suitable for performance with the means at his command. It may be that future generations will ransack the archives of St. George's as the archives of the Church of Saint Thomas have been ransacked, or as Sir George Grove rummaged Vienna in search of Schubert's early manuscripts. But for the present Mr. Elgar's early compositions are, to use his own words, suppressed, so none may predict the possibilities of the future.[13]

Buoyed up by a general critical approval of his most recent works, Elgar felt encouraged to suggest to Ivor Atkins – Done's successor at Worcester – that he should propose to the Executive Committee that Elgar be commissioned to furnish the forthcoming Three Choirs Festival with a new work. The general idea of suitability enshrined a concept of the heroic. Elgar's suggested subject – General Charles George Gordon – was approved. The accounts of the last days of Gordon's life, which had filled columns in the Worcester newspapers in January and February 1885, were well remembered. Gordon, a deeply religious man, was not only a martyr but (in a popular sense) a saint. As a wedding present Elgar had received from Father Knight, of St George's, a copy of Newman's *Gerontius*, with its original inscriptions by Frank Power, who had received it from Gordon.

On 25 February 1899 *The Athenaeum* announced that Elgar's new symphony for the 1899 Festival would bear the title 'Gordon'. With some prompting from Elgar the journalist described how 'the career of General Gordon, his martial achievements, restless energy, and religious fervour, have inspired the composer'. The passage ended with a reminder of 'Beethoven and his admiration of Napoleon, which led to the "Eroica" '. The *Sunday Times* of 5 March suggested that 'The work would form a dignified musical tribute to the memory of the revered soldier'.

In fact it did not. On 18 May the history of the 'Gordon' symphony effectively ended with an official notice of its withdrawal from the Worcester Festival, and in its place the *Light of Life* would be repeated. The reason for the withdrawal led to this comment:

> Mr. Elgar is just now extremely popular with his brother British musicians, owing to the withdrawal of his promised symphony from the Worcester Festival on the ground that the committee were not willing to pay properly for the work, £100 being the sum mentioned.[14]

By now Elgar's reputation was at the point of dramatic uplift. On 18 June Richter conducted the first performance of the 'Enigma' Variations, the effect of which was to convince the public of the presence of a quite original creative talent. The Variations had a narrative quality that in technical assurance, unmistakeable affiliation to the great European tradition, and with a startling luminosity of colouring, matched the endeavour of High Victorian art. Seven years of patient participation in Stockley's concerts had given insights into both Classical and Romantic instrumental techniques that could not otherwise have been gained.

It was after the production of Mendelssohn's *Elijah* at Birmingham in 1846 and the intellectual misconceptions supporting a Handel tradition, that oratorio in England, losing credibility as an art form, fell victim to the rigours of Protestantism and the Old Testament. The various Triennial Festivals were much to blame for this state of affairs, in that commissions for new works in this genre were not to be turned down by composers for whom alternative opportunities for earning money were scarce. Two composers stand out by reason of a degree of lively independence. Heinrich Hugo Pierson (born Henry Hugh Pearson), an expatriate conditioned by Spohr, Gounod, Meyerbeer, Schumann and Wagner, administered a sharp shock to the English system with *Jerusalem*, performed at Norwich in 1852. The conservatives disapproved and Pierson went back to Germany.

Alexander C Mackenzie, ten years older than Elgar – like him a violinist – was able to spend his impressionable student years in Germany. By conviction, he was a Scottish nationalist. In 1884 his oratorio, *The Rose of Sharon*, also given its first performance at the Norwich Festival, was greeted rapturously; he was showered with flowers by the chorus and accorded a 'standing ovation' by the audience. The subject, from the *Song of Songs*, was riotously secular, but Joseph Bennett, compiler of the libretto, judiciously attached to it a certification of morality by introducing 'a prologue suggesting the parabolic character of the drama, and an epilogue which points its moral'. Although oratorio became generally discredited through the conventional expectations of the commissioning committees, the occasions for such products 'were almost the only opportunities the Englishmen had of being heard by the great public'.[15]

Among Elgar's papers there remained one composition which under-writes the statement that he had considered Newman's *Dream* for eight years before considering setting it to music. A poem – *The tired Soul* – noted as written at Forli, belongs, therefore, to the years from 1891 to 1899.

> With the closing of the eyes
> Thought, out-wearied, heavenward flies;
>> Grows more ample, unrestrained,
>> Reaching to the unattained:
>>> Earthly littleness forgot,
>>> Petty strife concerns us not;
> Free the heart and mind arise,
> With the closing of the eyes.
> Then our loved ones, hand in hand,
> Wander with us in the land.
>> Where, – through golden seas of mist,
>> Shining woods and fields sunkissed, –
>>> Streams a wider deeper flow
>>> Of harmony than earth may know
> Tones too deep for us, unwise,
> Save with the closing of the eyes.
>
>   .   .   .   .   .   .
>
> 'Dreams' you say: – Alas! that we
> E'er must leave that shining sea.
>> Know again our care, distress,
>> Earth and all its littleness.
>>> But one day as slow time moves,
>>> Gathering up our dearest loves,
>>>> We shall pass from all the pain,
>>>> Burning heart and aching brain;
> Soon the fetter death unties,
> With the closing of the eyes.
>
> Forli   Edward Elgar

Elgar's final revision of the poem in typescript showed a different ending to that in the preceding manuscript version:

> Surely as the time now flies*
> Breaking dearest hopes and ties,*
> We may gather up our loves
> Our loves
>
> With the longed for last sweet sleep
> And closing of the weary eyes.[16]

Such a trochaic rhythmic pattern is familiar but infrequent; the internal rhyming scheme is unusual. Examples of this arrangement, intending to convey a sense of gravity, are to be found in religious verse; for example, in

A M Toplady's 'Rock of Ages', John Ellerton's 'Throned upon the awful tree', and Josiah Conder's 'Bread of heaven', all in *Hymns Ancient and Modern* (1861). The repeated 'closing of the eyes', appropriate to a death-bed, echoes H F Lyte's 'Abide with me'. Repetition of 'littleness' in the outer stanzas assists both design and sense, while the second stanza reflects a state of spiritual being in a pastoral setting encountered in, among others, Virgil, the Venerable Bede, Dante and Newman. The indication that a third stanza was omitted leaves a question unstated. There is also a suggestion of the climate and the colouring of Dante Gabriel Rossetti. 'Love's Nocturne' and 'Ave', for example, are instinct also with a refined sense of music.

But the poet most in Elgar's mind was, of course, Alice, and it is not difficult to believe that it was her poems, composed before their marriage, which were his inspiration. Concerning his (lost) Suite for Strings, of 1888, played at a Worcestershire Union Concert, its celebration remains in the climactic middle stanza of one of Alice's poems.

> But lo! they [the strains of the music] seem
> Hushed to a finer, mystic dream.
> The weaving rhythm of the song
> Ascends and bears the soul along.
> To loftier rapture must it soar
> Which sounds of earth can satisfy no more.

On New Year's Day 1900 George H Johnstone, chairman of the committee of the Birmingham Festival, came to Malvern to give the news that approval had been given for Elgar to compose a work based on *The Dream of Gerontius* for the forthcoming Festival. Next day Elgar confirmed by telegram his acceptance of the terms of the commission. Immediately he began to work again at what Alice described as a 'former libretto'.[17] In order to have permission to set passages from *Gerontius* Elgar consulted his friend Father Richard Bellasis. He advised him to approach Father William Neville, who had joined Newman in the earliest days of the Oratory, had acted for him as his secretary, and had been with him at the time of his death. In response to Elgar's letter of 6 January Neville asked that Elgar should visit him at the Oratory. In suggesting a day, Elgar still appeared uncertain as to whether the Festival Committee might not countermand Johnstone's acceptance of the subject.

> I am hoping to be in Birmingham on Friday & should be very much obliged if you cd. spare time for a short interview: I am not sure if the Committee will approve of the subject: I should naturally have to shorten, *not alter* anything & I should of course not omit anything peculiar to our Catholic point of view but w^d prefer to talk this over with you.
>
> As to copyright – in case other points are settled – this of course remains in the owners' hands permission being sought only to print the words with music.[18]

Elgar duly went to the Oratory and agreed with Neville the matter of permission to use the text. Permission was duly forthcoming, on condition that it only applied to those parts of the poem which were set to music. There was to be a fee of ten guineas or one penny on each copy of the words printed in programme books.

That Elgar could, at the beginning of January, begin the composition of a major and complex work which would have its first performance nine months later is, to say the least, remarkable. His only competitor in respect of quick results was Handel. Both composers were past masters at making use of previously considered material – in Elgar's case, his own. With rare exceptions – of the 'Gordon' symphony and the Leeds symphony commission of 1904 – Elgar had an eighteenth-century attitude to contracts. In this respect the tradesman's son, he fulfilled his commissions on time.

The timetable for *Gerontius* is clearly marked in Alice's diary and in correspondence. Very little is known as to material which came to *Gerontius* from previous sketches. Among earlier material left aside, there is one theme which was written into George Sinclair's guest-book in Hereford: the amusing motif of Dan (Sinclair's bull dog) of 19–20 April 1898, which – when motifs were labelled in the analysis published to accompany the first performance – came to denote 'prayer'. The *Andantino* which commences at figure 12 he acknowledged as coming from the 'Gordon' project.[19]

On 5 February, noting that arrangements for the commission had been settled with Birmingham, Elgar described the poem to Jaeger as 'awfully solemn & mystic'. He was by now far enough into the work to be able to end his letter by noting his intention to go on with his 'Devil's chorus' and to use a 'Judas' motif 'for death & despair in this work'.[20] On 7 February the 'Enigma' Variations were given their first performance in Birmingham by the Halle Orchestra, with Richter conducting. Next day the Elgars went to Manchester for a repeat performance and to have dinner with Richter.

On 2 March four pages of short score (to figure 35) went to Novello. Anticipating an official anouncement of the commissioning of *Gerontius* the *Leeds Mercury* indicated its disapproval with an oblique note of Protestant distaste:

> Newman's poem does not exactly 'yearn' for musical treatment, but there are many possibilities about it, and Mr. Elgar, who may be described as in thorough sympathy with the poet and his views, can be trusted to make the utmost of them.

Across spring and early summer the work was brought together section by section. The original manuscript sheets went from Birchwood Lodge – the leafy retreat near Malvern where Elgar preferred to compose – to

London, the engraved sheets returning for correction or alteration.[17] By June, Elgar, now working hard and orchestrating the work, was able to save time by pasting sections from the vocal staves of the printed score on to his progressing MS full score. Those days are vividly restored by two observations written by Elgar into the full score: three bars after figure 15 – below . . . 'from earth to heaven', 'at Birchwood Lodge in Summertime'; and below the score at figure 42 '. . . Like beasts of prey', 'Birchwood Lodge / in Thunderstorm'. On 6 June Alice noted: 'E finished the Dream of Gerontius. Deo gratias. Rather poorly'. Orchestrating the work was completed on 3 August.

On 6 April Elgar had spent part of the day working on the text of *Gerontius* with Father Ralph Blakelock of the Oratory.[21] In his subsequent communications to Jaeger, Elgar exposed a strong commitment to the theological significance of the text. On 13 April Jaeger wondered how Elgar would deal with that part of the poem taking the soul of Gerontius into the Presence of the Almighty. Elgar responded:

> Please remember that none of the 'action' takes place in the *presence* of God: I would not have tried *that* neither did Newman. The Soul says 'I go before my God', but *we* don't. We stand outside – I've thrown over all the 'machinery' the celestial music, harps etc.

When, on 14 June, in order to discourage antagonism to the work on sectarian grounds, Jaeger wondered whether 'we can remove Mary & Joseph to a more distant background', Elgar immediately replied:

> As to the Catholic side, of course it will frighten the low Church party but the poem must on no account be touched! Sacrilege and not to be thought of: them as don't like it can be damned in their own way – not ours. It's awfully curious the attitude (towards sacred things) of the narrow English mind . . . .

On 30 June, in a long letter concerning various technical suggestions, Elgar chided Jaeger for a lack of appreciation. At rehearsal figure 120 the score states, ' "for one moment" must every instrument exert its fullest force', after which Elgar urges,

> you must read the poem: I cannot rewrite this: the Soul is shrivelled up & voiceless & I only want on this page a musing murmur & I've got it – it wakes up later – but I can't do better if I try for fifty years.

The last cry of the Soul, '. . . take me away, and in the lowest deep / There let me be', descends against a background of high strings. The Souls in Purgatory begin to intone Psalm 90, and cellos and basses (with timpani) enter *pppp*. In the full score Elgar indicates, 'the murmurando close & with very little bow'.

On 27 June Elgar came back to the same passage:

> I've kept p. 159 back for consideration, but all the time I know I'm right
> & that you're wrong. However, I'll see – one thing does annoy me. You say
> I've 'shirked' it' – now I've shirked nothing – I've only set the thing as I feel
> & see it, which is not shirking at all, at all . . .

This reply is in harmony with Newman's answer to John Telford: 'I have
said only what I saw'.

Elgar's most significant theological observation is perhaps contained in a
letter of August in respect of Jaeger's preparation of an analysis of the
work for the *The Musical Times*. 'My wife', wrote Elgar, 'fears you may be
inclined to lay too great stress on the leitmotiven plan because I really do it
without thought – intuitively, I mean'.

> Look here: I imagined Gerontius to be a man like us not a priest or a
> saint, but a *sinner*, a repentant one of course but still no end of a *wordly man*
> in his life, & now brought to book. Therefore I've not filled his part with
> Church tunes & rubbish but a good, healthy full-blooded romantic,
> remembered worldliness, so to speak. It is, I imagine, much more difficult to
> tear one's self away from a well to do world than from a cloister.

In the sermon 'Moral Consequences and Single Sins' Newman characteristically used his own musical experience with which to elucidate his
argument:

> . . . there is a fault out of sight He [the sinner] forgets, that in spite of this
> harmony between all within and all without for twenty-three hours of the
> day, there is one subject, now and then recurring, which jars with his mind –
> there is just one string out of tune.[22]

In three quotations on the autograph score of *Gerontius* Elgar suggested
philosophical consideration of the idea of the transient soul in three
quotations bearing a wide range of intellectual concepts. Two, which are
inter-related, are on the title page, indicating the remarkable breadth of
Elgar's literary exploration. Both concern concepts of the soul, arising out
of the question asked by Aeneas of his father Anchises in the Sixth Book of
Virgil's *Aeneid*: 'Quae lucis miseris tam dira cupido?'

The same question – twice translated – is given in *The Essays of
Montaigne / done into English / by John Florio, 1603*[23] as: 'Whence doth
so dyre desire of light on wretches grow?'

Aeneas has met his father Anchises in the underworld, in a green valley.
He is taken by Anchises to the banks of the Lethe where souls, envisaged in
human form, await return to another life on earth. 'Why should they so
fearfully wish for the light of our day?' Anchises' answer to this question,
long and complex, owes much to legends and theologies, and to poets and
philosophers, of the ancient world. Central to the answer is the Platonic
concept of *metempsychosis* – transmigration of the soul. He tells how after
death the departing soul does not leave the world entirely free either of evil

or bodily ills; that on account of these defects there is due punishment; that the cleansing of tainted souls is by water or by fire. If there is a sight of hell, then there is a view of heaven and also of purgatory. Virgil's vision carried across the Middle Ages.

It was not surprising, therefore, that during the Renaissance, when new answers to old questions were sought, Virgil's texts underwent fresh examination. Montaigne was one of the most widely read essayists of the late sixteenth century. He was prolific in the beguiling presentation of new ideas, from which he would remain detached, unwilling to arrive at conclusions.[24]

On the subject of the soul, Virgil was but one of many classical authorities cited by Montaigne. To Elgar's association with Virgil there is a revealing phrase in a letter to him from A C Benson, after hearing a performance of *The Apostles* in King's College Chapel, Cambridge:

> You are a great magician, like Berlioz, like Virgil. I do envy you the source of joy. Of course I know that the conception and creation of a beautiful thing is not without sorrow and pain . . . .[25]

Elgar, beside the Malvern Hills, was moved by William Langland's visionary tale of Piers Plowman, and by the truth within that Dream. At the end of his score, Elgar placed his third quotation, from Ruskin's *Sesame and Lilies*:

> This is the best of me: for the rest, I ate and drank, and slept, lived, and hated, like another; my life was as the vapour, and is not; but *this* I saw and knew: this, if anything of mine is worth your memory.

Elgar returns to an absolute: 'This I saw and knew', balancing Newman's 'I have said what I saw'.

In retrospect, it is remarkable that the Birmingham Festival Committee approved the choice of *The Dream of Gerontius* for the 1900 Festival. The composer was, in their view, well enough qualified to write the music for a work which, if not an oratorio, would give some appearance of belonging to that genre. As with opera in the eighteenth century, the nature of a libretto, more often than not, was a matter of indifference. But Newman's poem had within it the seeds of politico-religious divisiveness.

It now seems optimistic that a work of the complexity of Elgar's *Gerontius* could have been put into choral rehearsal in July with the hope of adequate performance at the beginning of October. The death of Swinnerton Heap, chorus master for the Birmingham Festival, on 11 June, was a considerable blow, for he was well acquainted with Elgar and his style. His replacement was Stockley, recalled from retirement. But it was clear that the choir simply was not good enough. The first performamce of *Gerontius* on 3 October was – so far as Elgar was concerned – catastrophic. The *Observer* was quite clear as to where responsibility lay:

The Birmingham choir is no longer a body of vocalists to which an Englishman can point with pride. In 1897 the constant false intonation was attributed to the adoption of the *diapason normal* and to over zeal in weeding out choristers whose voices were no longer fresh, but who were reliable sight-readers. These were excuses, however, that only testified to faulty system and imperfect preparation, the results of which this year have been still more painfully apparent . . . .

. . . Dr. Richter is an orchestral conductor *par excellence*, but his ability to direct performances of English oratorio is open to question . . . . The shortcomings of the choir were specially to be regretted, because Mr. Edward Elgar's sacred cantata, *The Dream of Gerontius*, the outcome of eight years' thought, and a choral masterpiece, was presented in so faulty and pointless a manner as to seriously jeopardise its success.[26]

Against the bitterness which Elgar felt, and expressed, there was consolation in the assurances he received. Among them was a thoughtful letter from Huw Powell, 'HDHP' of the Enigma Variations:

> United University
> Club,
> Pall Mall East, S.W.
> Sunday evg.

My dear Elgar:

I must take advantage of the first spare moment I have had since I got home on Friday Night, to send you a few lines – In one way they are to console you on the very poor treatment which the Birmingham choir gave to your beautiful work. I was afraid what would happen when I heard the muddle that the choir made of Parry's work on Tuesday evening. I don't know where the fault lay, but with all my experience (nearly thirty years) of Birmingham Festival performance I never heard the choir sing, through the whole festival with rare exceptions, worse.

The tenors seemed incapable of keeping to pitch even in the simplest passages: and often during the performance of 'Gerontius' I found myself wishing that the choir would stop altogether and let me hear the wonderfully beautiful passages which you have given to the orchestra – I could only imagine what the vocal part ought to sound like, and long for some capable singers to do justice to the most moving & sometimes overpowering choral work you have written.

You seem to me to have just caught the right spirit of the poem and I was very deeply impressed – your setting of the words of the Angel of the Passion appears to me, at least on paper, in a different way with the Lament of Caractacus; and the music of the Guardian Angel is as beautiful and appropriate as could be written – in fact I don't know where to stop in my admiration! I can only say that all lovers of music should feel that they owe you a huge debt of gratitude. I sincerely hope that one of these days (and may it be soon!) I shall hear the work again & done in a more worthy manner. Were you present on Friday morning? The Choir seemed to have recovered themselves a little in the Requiem, but even there they were not by any means immaculate.

But the wonderful performance of the 7th Symphony at the end of the programme compensated for much. I hope you are taking a rest after all the excitement, and are not feeling the iniquities of the Chorus too deeply

My kindest regards to your wife

Ever y[rs] sincerely
Huw D.S. Powell

I have just been to see poor Basil [Nevinson]. (He is desperately gouty & very low about himself, but is still keeping on the right road to recovery I rejoice to say.[27]

There was also a significant letter of appreciation from Bishop Ilsley.

Oscott College / Birmingham / Oct 10th 1900

My dear Mr Elgar:

During the past week I fear you have been overwhelmed with correspondence following the production of your 'Dream of Gerontius' at the Birmingham Festival. But now that you have had a breathing space I hope you will allow me, as your diocesan, to offer you my very sincere and hearty congratulations on the success you have achieved. It was a bold undertaking to set to music that sublime poem of the illustrious Cardinal. And I confess that I went to the Festival with a certain misgiving as to the possibility of any musical setting doing justice to the poem. As it proceeded however my fears vanished; for it was evident you had entered with all your soul into the treating of the subject, and were employing the ample resources at your command to give it worthy expression. In this age of materialism it is no small matter to have called the attention of thousands to a poem which described the death bed scene of a Christian & the journey into the other world so truthfully and graphically. More than this you have added to it a new charm which will enhance it in the eyes of the musical world, to so many of whom the poem was a sealed book. In this respect your work is a triumph of faith, on which I once more sincerely congratulate you.

Believe me
Yours very faithfully in Xt,
X Edward Bp of Birmingham

Mr Elgar
Great Malvern[28]

An appreciation of the work in the November 1900 issue of *The Musical Times* was in agreement with the Bishop's main conclusion:

'The Dream of Gerontius' is a work of great originality, beauty, and power; and, above all, of the completest sincerity. It is not desirable, of course, to introduce theological notions into the discussion of a composition; but it is necessary to refer to the fact that no one but a Catholic could approach Cardinal Newman's poem in the right spirit.[29]

A decade later, Birmingham became an archdiocese and Ilsley became the first archbishop. His Investiture took place on 8 November in St Chad's Cathedral. The Master of Ceremony was Rev D Sheil, the Deacon of the Mass, Rev R O Eaton, both Fathers of the Oratory and keen Elgarians.[30] The Presentation of the Jubilee Vestments was made at a ceremony in the Town Hall. On arrival the new archbishop was greeted by a combined male voice choir, singing the same *Ecce sacerdos magnus*, of Elgar, which had greeted him in St George's Church, Worcester in 1888.

Notes

1   Fr Fawkes, b 1849, ordained 1880, left the Oratory 1890.
2   Cliffe's First Symphony was looked at with some favour, but was not selected for the Leeds Festival of that year, because 'the managers of the Yorkshire meeting questioned the propriety of producing an extended work by a young composer whose name would be little known to musical people of remote districts'. His Second Symphony was performed at the Leeds Festival of 1892 (6 October), and at a Stockley Concert on 2 March 1893.
3   Children of Elgar's sister Susanna Mary (Polly) and William Grafton.
4   Young, *Letters of Edward Elgar*, pp 58–60.
5   Moore, *Letters of a Lifetime*, 1990, p 40.
6   *The Musical Courier*, London, 19 November 1896.
7   Moore, *Edward Elgar: A Creative Life*, p 177.
8   *Birmingham Post*, 30 October 1893.
9   *Coventry Herald and Free Press*, 25 November 1893.
10   *Birmingham Daily Gazette*, 17 December 1895.
11   *Worcester Herald*, 7 November 1896.
12   *The Musician*, 15 September 1897; the *St James's Gazette* praised 'many fine passages' but, noting the influence of Wagner, deplored a lack of 'religious feeling'.
13   *Yorkshire Post*, 5 March 1898.
14   *The Daily Post*, c 15 September 1899.
15   Fuller-Maitland, J A, *A Doorkeeper of Music*, p 14.
16   Young, *Alice Elgar*, Dennis Dobson, 1978, p 184.
17   Diary, 2 January 1900.
18   Fee settled, 14 June.
19   Moore, *Edward Elgar: A Creative Life*, OUP, 1984, p 246.
20   Ibid, p 295; the 'Judas' theme was with sketches for an oratorio on the subject of the Apostles, which (without this theme) came in 1903.
21   Blakelock succeeded Newman as Superior, d 1904, was succeeded by Ignatius Ryder, d 1907.
22   *Selection of Parochial and Plain Sermons*, xxxix for Sundays after Trinity, p 337.
23   *The Essays of Montaigne / done into English / by John Florio 1603*, G Sainsbury's edition, London 1892: Montaigne's translation of a 'Tale of

Raymond Sebord, Professor at Toulouse', author of *Theologia naturala*, trans Montaigne, 1569; Florio (1553?–1625), son of an Italian Protestant refugee; published Italian–English dictionary in 1598, in 1603 Reader in Italian to Queen Anne.

24   Elton, W R, 'Shakespeare and the Thought of his Age', *The Cambridge Companion to Shakespeare Studies*, ed Stanley Wells, Cambridge 1986, p 26.

25   Benson, A C, HWRO:445:3747, 24 June 1906.

26   *Observer*, 7 October 1900.

27   HWRO 445:3696; Basil Nevinson = BGN of 'Enigma' Variation XIII.

28   HWRO 445:3676.

29   *Mus T*, vol 44, 1903, p 477.

30   *Mus T*, vol 75, 1934, p 638, report of a presentation to Father Robert Eaton in token of his ten year conductorship of the Birmingham Catholic Choir, which has 'done much for the understanding and appreciation of the finest polyphonic music'.

10 '. . . Sundry Ejaculations'

On the morning of 17 October 1900 Alice Elgar sent for Rosa Burley, friend of the family, who was thought in an emergency to have some influence over Elgar. She duly arrived at Craeg Lea – the house to which the Elgars had moved during the previous year. Elgar was in his upstairs study.

> I went up cautiously and found him sitting at his table with his head in his hand. He said gloomily, 'They've offered me a Doctor's Degree at Cambridge University, but I shan't accept it. I'm just writing a refusal'.

> *Miss B*: Won't accept it, but why not?
> *Elgar*: It's too late.
> *Miss B*: Too late, for what?
> *Elgar*: For everything.
> *Miss B*: I don't understand it. Why it is the greatest honour they can offer you. This is a recognition of Gerontius. You can't snub Cambridge University.[1]

The session ended, of course, with Elgar recovered from this attack of self-doubt and writing his letter of acceptance.

On St Cecilia's Day the Elgars and friend duly attended at Senate House for the congregation. As well as Elgar, Frederick Cowen (whose works frequently appeared on Stockley's Programmes at Birmingham) also received an honorary degree. Although the honours had been decreed some time before the occasion, the public orator was well up to date with his reference to *Gerontius*.

> . . . He has recently described in musical terms the gentle fall – through an infinity of space and in the smallest interval of time – of the soul [of Gerontius] while celestial choirs sing 'Praise God in the highest. Praise God in the depth'. At the same time this is accompanied most worthily with the varied harmonies of the orchestra . . . .[2]

Added to this was a singularly apt sentence in Greek from Homer's *Odyssey*, a minstrel pleading for his life begins to address Odysseus: 'Self-taught am I, and the god has planted in my heart all manner of songs, and worthy am I to sing to thee as to a god . . .'

John Edwin Sandys, a Classical scholar of eminence who served as public orator at Cambridge from 1876 to 1919, was renowned for the elegant style of his presentations. Reporting the events of the day to her mother-in-law Alice Elgar noted that Edward — no doubt somewhat roguishly — had been able to criticize the Latin (pronunciation?) of the public orator, who was reported to have been amused. Purchasing the appropriate robes for the honour had been a problem for the impoverished Elgars. Fortunately it was solved by subscriptions from friends.

The opportunity for the musical public of the City and County of Worcestershire to recognize the distinction accorded to Elgar came on 9 May 1901, at the spring concert of the County Philharmonic Society. The first half of the programme consisted of the Overture and Prize Song from the *Meistersänger, Sea Pictures*, and a Romance and Bolero by J W Austin, leader of the orchestra — 'honest John' as Elgar called him. He conducted his own piece, so that for this item Elgar led the second violins. The second half of the programme consisted of a reduced version of *The Dream*, the singers being William Greene (Gerontius), Helen Vulna (Angel) and F Lightowler (Priest). How the composer thought his work should be received is indicated in the account of the performance in the *Worcester Herald* of 11 May.

> *Gerontius*, though it was only heard in part, created a really profound impression. One could quite understand Dr Elgar's objection to any applause between the parts, and even at the end. It seems something of a desecration of the religious spirit which pervades the work, though, of course, everyone was anxious to let the composer know how deeply he had stirred them by the wonderful beauty and mysticism with which he has treated the great poem.

During this year the theme of death was at the climax of Elgar's music for *Grania and Diarmid*, his contribution to the cause of Irish nationalism. At the beginning of 1902 the idea of dreams — now through the gentle, sad thoughts of Charles Lamb — germinated in *Dream Children*. On 20 May of that year Elgar recorded what was, perhaps, the single most significant success of his career: *The Dream of Gerontius* was performed at the Düsseldorf Music Festival in Germany and as a result Elgar was received into the European musical community. Richard Strauss, speaking of *Gerontius* on this occasion, decreed: 'With that work England for the first time became one of the modern musical states'.

The critic Max Hehemann, having first noticed that England was not seriously to be considered by Germans as a homeland of composers, went on to say how much greater, therefore, was the impact made by 'The Dream of Gerontius' which:

> . . . in its expression of the particular spirit of Catholicism is one of the most notable examples in modern music. In this connection the music of the angelic choirs, from time to time, is to be compared with Palestrina. I must then retract what I have said previously in respect of Elgar. For he is an entirely modern composer, a man who goes his own way.[3]

Prior to this the threat of problems ahead had begun to take uncomfortable shape. At the Gloucester Festival of 1901 only the Prelude and 'Angel's Farewell' were performed, so that the whole work was due for its first performance at a Three Choirs Festival at Worcester, in the following September. That there could be difficulties regarding those passages in the text concerning Invocations to the Blessed Virgin Mary and the Saints seems to have been understood by Ivor Atkins, who talked on the subject with Canon T L Claughton – a residentiary canon and chairman of the Executive Committee of the Festival – as well as with Elgar early in 1902. It then appears that the matter was put to the newly arrived, and already exhausted, Bishop of Worcester, Charles Gore.[4]

A leading member of the Anglo-Catholic branch of the church, Gore had been a Fellow of Trinity College, Oxford, Principal of Pusey House, and founder of the Community of the Resurrection. His nomination to a traditionally Protestant see, therefore, was unwelcome to many in the diocese of Worcester. As editor of *Lux Mundi*, a collection of essays by a group of theologians teaching at Oxford between 1875 and 1885, he incurred the anger of extremists with his definition of the book's aim: 'to put the Catholic Faith into its right relation to modern intellectual and moral problems'. He had also alienated himself from staunch imperialists with a letter to *The Times* in November, 1901, critical of the government's conduct of the South African war. When Gore's nomination was announced a Protestant journal called on loyal churchmen to pray, 'O God, have mercy on this Romaniser'. Opponents within the Church Association took their protest to the highest level of ecclesiastical jurisdiction. Finally all objections were dismissed, but Gore's consecration, which should have taken place in January 1902, was delayed until February.

Thus the matter of the suitability of the text of *The Dream of Gerontius* for a musical performance in the cathedral was not one that he would have welcomed. When the matter was brought to him the bishop temporized. After a meeting of the Festival Executive Committee on 12 April – at which Elgar was present – had taken place, it was decided to postpone any action. A week later Atkins visited Elgar, and on 24 April – on a day when Lady Mary Lygon came to tea – Canon Claughton called.

Elgar promised to refer the problem of the text to Father Richard Bellasis, to whom he wrote on 27 April:

> You know Gerontius is down for the Worcester Festival; my clerical friends do not *mind* i.e. object to the subject & it passed committee without cavil. Now some objector has written to the Bishop & has stirred up strife: the committee has drawn up a list of such *omission* of words, <which the Bishop> if it is permissible to make such omissions the Bishop will sanction or countenance the performance. These omissions will be made only in the book of the words sold in the cathedral & I sh^d suggest the heading 'the words selected from a poem by Cardinal Newman'. The objectors will not have the litany of the saints & sundry ejaculations.
>
> Now; will you tell me if the owners of the copyright – who have already given Novello, as publisher general use of the words – will *tacitly* allow the plan.
>
> *I* do not sanction any change – I merely concur & the responsibility of making such change rests with the authorities.
>
> Please let me know what you think & you will forgive me for troubling you I know. If this performance takes place it will be a great thing for the work & it may then be allowed to take its place in peace.
>
> It must be understood that *no* edition of the music with alteration is contemplated – merely for the Cathedral book of words.[5]

On 15 May the *Birmingham Post* published what it had learned about the matter in an article headed 'Worcester Musical Festival – A Difficulty Solved'. Within the Festival Executive Committee it is clear that much time had been devoted to discussion of 'certain words and the expression of sentiments which it is thought were such as should not be sung in the Cathedral'. Eventually, it seemed, a solution was reached by the Dean and Chapter and the Committee, who – after consultation with Elgar – agreed to 'an omission and some slight alterations'.

Father Bellasis, reading the forbidden word 'alteration' asked Elgar exactly what was happening to the text of the *Dream*. On the eve of going to Düsseldorf Elgar wrote to Jaeger, explaining the difficulty at Worcester:

> . . . what is proposed is to omit the litany of the saints – to substitute other words for Mary & Joseph – & to put 'Souls' only over the chorus at the end instead of 'Souls in Purgatory' & to put 'prayers' instead of Masses in the Angel's Farewell. The point is that (quite unfairly I feel) Atkins &c. expect *me* to take the responsibility & I promised to enquire for *authority* for them to do it as they wish. So far I have only said I have no objection to the alterations or that I concur – permission I cannot give.[6]

After the Festival Committee had discussed the matter of the libretto for *Gerontius* it had been taken up by Ivor Atkins. He had, it appears, shown a draft revision to Father Neville, about which Canon Claughton wrote to Elgar.

> I don't know whether Atkins has told you, that, in reply to our inquiring

about the copyright of the book of your beautiful work Novello & Co have written to say that they can accept no responsibility whatever for any alterations or omissions which must rest entirely with the Executive Committee. They add that any exception w^d be taken by the owners of the copyright to omission, they w^d not be likely to take the same view with regard to alterations.

As you are aware the latter are very slight in point of number – only two I believe – the substitution of 'Jesu' for 'Maria' in one place, & of 'Prayers on the Earth' for 'Masses on the Earth' in another.

But if exception were taken to these alterations in our books afterwards, would it, do you think, meet the objections of the owners if we were to omit the words in question altogether from the books of words?

It makes me very anxious now that the time is so near to have no question of this important nature still unsettled. You have been so exceptionally kind about the whole thing & so considerate, that I am loth to trouble you again in the matter.

But I hope you will forgive me if I ask you whether you could possibly do anything towards the solution of this, the only remaining difficulty, in person, or failing that, whether you w^d be good enough to advise us, at your earliest convenience, how best to proceed.

The avidity with which the public, to judge by yesterday's issue of tickets, are looking forward to hearing the work makes me doubly anxious to have everything satisfactorily settled with the least possible delay. We shall be very grateful if you can help us.[7]

It seeming that all was well in respect of the text, the next weeks followed purposefully. For many years it had been the custom to import some professional choralists from the northern towns most celebrated in this respect. But recently the Leeds choristers had lost credit.[8] So, for the first time in recent years the chorus for the Festival was to be drawn only from the three cathedral cities. There were, however, difficulties to be settled in respect of the availability of soloists, and it took a little time to find three who were free and also had adequate experience of Elgar. Finally, Muriel Foster, John Coates and Plunket Greene were engaged.

The orchestra for the Festival was recruited from among the best-known London professionals and was led by W Frye Parker. In 1902 the twenty-six year-old W H Reed – one of the first violins of Henry Wood's Queen's Hall Orchestra – was playing for a Three Choirs Festival for the first time. He was to become Elgar's friend and a familiar, cheerful figure at the festivals for many years to come. A preliminary rehearsal with orchestra and soloists always took place in London in the week preceding the Festival. On September 2 Atkins took the orchestra through its programme.

Berrow's Journal sent a member of the staff to cover the rehearsal. It was the first time he had heard any of *Gerontius*, of which, he wrote, 'the music possesses an extraordinary amount of idealism, and conveys the inner meaning of the subject of the poem'. With music which they thought of as familiar the players relaxed. But Atkins was equal to the challenge:

> Matters did not progress so smoothly at the afternoon practice, where the Beethoven [Fifth] symphony was taken through. Mr. Atkins is anxious to secure his own rendering of the work, and, as the members of the orchestra have fallen into a more or less conventional manner of playing this symphony, it was necessary to get them out of it, which he did.[9]

To Elgar's great distress, his mother, who had been his first source of inspiration and confidence, died during the night of 1 September. The funeral took place three days later. At the last rehearsal before the Festival Elgar told the choristers how one of her last wishes was that he should not withdraw from conducting *Gerontius*.

By this time Elgar had made a profoundly important decision.

Craeg Lea, August 8 1902

My dear Father Bellasis:

> My original M.S. Full Score of Gerontius will probably, now that the whole score is printed, be my property – the publishers will give it to me if I ask for it. Can you tell me if the Oratory w^d accept it & give it place of rest somewhere near to where the revered Cardinal lived? Please do not say anything officially – I should like your own private opinion – if this is favourable I would ask the publishers – if they concur I would formally offer the M.S. to the Oratory Library: – but you may think it not worth while to be bothered with it

> > With kindest regards
> > Believe me
> > Ever sincerely yours,
> > Edward Elgar[10]

Elgar added a postscript which carries a special significance. Here he acknowledges a reverence for Newman as priest, and acknowledges his own spiritual identity within Gerontius

> I must add that nothing would give me greater happiness than to feel that the work, into which I put my whole soul, sh^d be in its original form, near to where the sacred author of the poem made his influence felt.

The first Three Choirs Festival of the twentieth century had begun under a general sense of elation; an age of peace and prosperity might have idly now been anticipated. This should have been an ideal opportunity for the new bishop to deliver an appropriate message. In fact, on the opening day of the Festival, he did not preach the sermon that had been anticipated. It was Canon Knox-Little who ascended the pulpit, to announce that 'the

Bishop was prevented from preaching by indisposition which they all hoped would be short, and that he himself would deliver the sermon'.

To hear *Gerontius*, on Thursday 11 September, there was both a full and a fashionable audience in the cathedral. Most of the nobility of three counties was present as well as a number of political figures. Among these were the young Stanley Baldwin, who had recently been the unsuccessful Conservative candidate for Kidderminster, and his wife. Baldwin remained a friend of the Festival, and of Worcestershire composers, throughout his life.

After the performance Alice Elgar noted: 'A most wonderful day to have had in one's life'. To this she added on the next day, 'Overwhelming joy of everyone about Gerontius'.[11] It was the first time Elgar had conducted the work in one of the Three Choirs Cathedrals.

He received many messages of congratulation on the performance. Perhaps the most charmingly heartfelt was from a nurse at St George's Hospital in London:

Dear Dr Elgar:

I have just had 24 hours' leave of absence from my work & rushed down to hear 'Gerontius'. And as I didn't see you to speak one word to you on that very busy day, I want to write the word I should have liked to speak, & say, namely, that it was heavenly. I have been very keen to hear it, and this was my first chance. And one can't help feeling very angry & truly ashamed (if one may tell you so) that there should have been any sort of question about it, or that there could exist in anybody a feeling which prompts discussion, alteration, or omission. This tribute both for Newman & you!

Please excuse the pencil as this is written during tea.

Yours truly

Winifred Broome[12]

Father Denis Sheil, the last novice to have been admitted to the Oratory by Newman, wrote:

The Oratory, Sept 12 1902

Dear Dr Elgar:

I have not had the pleasure of meeting your personally, but as you know several of our Fathers, I thought I might venture to tell you how profoundly I admire your Gerontius. I heard it two years ago, and was deeply moved by it, in spite of the injustice that the execution did to it. But after first hearing it again this morning, I feel it is an absolutely *worthy* rendering of the Cardinal's idea. Father Eaton who was with me, is as enthusiastic and I know how we all of us congratulate ourselves that the work has found an adequate (I use the word in strict letter) expression in music.

Of course I am nobody, and my opinion as a critic worthless, and I only venture to tell you this because I write from here.

> Believe me,
>
> > Yours faithfully,
> > Denis Sheil[13]

Of all the members of the Oratory community, Robert Eaton, who spent a great part of his life as choral conductor, was the best qualified to express an opinion on music. He wrote to Elgar on 14 September:

> May I be allowed as one who lives in the house where Gerontius was written, to again thank you for your superb musical setting of the poem – and to congratulate you very warmly on the rendering of your work last Thursday at Worcester? I was present and enjoyed it to the full. The intonation and quality of tone of the chorus were all one could wish – and surely Miss Foster is a true artist. I had heard the work mutilated at its first production here – and do indeed rejoice that at last it has received a good rendering in England. I wish I could express all I feel about Gerontius – and how I would like to go through the score some day with you to explain it more fully to me. I will pray that you may long be spared to write . . . .[14]

On 21 September Richard Bellasis wrote to Elgar that 'the priceless treasure' of the manuscript had arrived at the Oratory. On 8 October he wrote again, giving the resolution passed that morning by the Fathers:

> That the best thanks of the Congregation are due to Dr Elgar for his very valuable and interesting present of the original full-score MS of 'The Dream of Gerontius'. The Fathers desire to put on record their hearty appreciation of Dr Elgar's brilliant success in the work he has accomplished, as well as of the spirit of genuine devotion to Cardinal Newman's memory and Poem which inspired the undertaking, and has prompted the presentation to the Oratory of the original score of the work.[15]

In the *Birmingham Post* of 12 September there had appeared a long and brilliant review of *Gerontius*, in which the 'difficulty that had been solved' was subtly alluded to. The Prelude to the work

> . . . prepared the mind for the proper mood in which to hear that wonderful soul-picture of the process of dying, with faith on the one side, and shrinking weakness on the other, pleading for the intercession of the Virgin Mother, of saints and angels. It is true there were excisions of the text and some words were substituted for others, but the author's conception was there and the composer has expressed it in a manner impossible to one who did not feel the truth of it.

In the light of the record of misadventures, in respect of the use of Latin texts, that had occurred in the cathedral during previous Festivals, what happened in Worcester after the performance of *Gerontius* in 1902 should have been predictable.

In 1836 it was enjoined that Mozart's *Requiem* – to achieve respectability – should be freshly titled *Redemption* and supplied both with English words, by Edward Taylor, and additional non-Mozartian music. This, to their credit, 'justly excited the opposition of the critics'.[16] In the same meeting Miss Maria Hawes was required to substitute English words for the original of Cherubini's *O salutaris*, while Clara Novello's hope of singing Cherubini's *Ave Maria* and Hummel's *Alma Virgo* without alteration was likewise frustrated. Miss Novello was, moreover, commended for the 'amiable manner and readiness with which she consented to substitute other pieces [by Handel and Haydn] for those previously chosen'. To suit Protestant susceptibilities, at Gloucester in 1850, Beethoven's Mass in C was disguised as a 'service'.

Regarding the Worcester performance of 1902, the consequence of the attempt to cleanse Newman's text was noticed by the Rev T A Burge OSB in *The Tablet*:

> . . . There was one jar, and that a particularly disagreeable one in the action of the Festival Committee, who did not shrink from censuring Cardinal Newman's exquisite poem. The beautiful number containing the prayers for the dying, 'Holy Mary, pray for him', was suppressed, the ejaculations of the poor soul to our Blessed Lady were either omitted, or other words substituted. No exception seems to have been taken to the 'cleansing fires' of Purgatory, but the reference to 'Masses on earth' was not allowed to fall from the singer's lips. The annoyance felt in the audience was unmistakeable; it was galling enough to Catholics; and the musical critics of *The Times* and *The Telegraph* expressing the feelings of the profession, have condemned the mutilations in the severest terms.[17]

In the October issue of the *Catholic Monthly Register* it was observed that the attendance at the 1902 Festival, of 19,100 people represented a falling-off from the two previous Festivals, but that the largest attendance during the week (anticipated by the Dean, with satisfaction, in his letter to Elgar of 22 July) was for *Gerontius*. This was probably why, the paper suggested, the Festival Committee had agreed to include the work in their programme. The *Register* was severe in its criticism of the alterations made to Newman's poem. quoting Canon Teignmouth Shore that it was an act of 'literary vandalism'.[18] The absurdities that resulted were outlined by J A Fuller Maitland in his volume of recollections:

> The soloists were required . . . to mumble the name 'Maria' at the beginning of the tenor solo, and at the words 'and masses on the earth and prayers in heaven' the representative of the angel must sing the first words with closed lips.[19]

In 1905 at Worcester *Elijah* was moved from Tuesday morning to Thursday evening to make room for *Gerontius*, in the performance of which the *Musical World* noticed that,

> certain references to the Virgin had been expunged and to that extent the work was mutilated. Later, Mozart's 'Requiem' was given in its entirety, but perhaps that was because it was sung in Latin.

But this was by no means the end of the affair. In 1908 the *Yorkshire Post*, reporting the Worcester Festival of that year, observed:

> The modifications of the text introduced to bring it into touch with Anglican doctrine were employed, and that reasonably enough as long as these Oratorio performances are given in an Anglican Cathedral, and under the guise of services. But it was impossible not to be struck by the fact that the prayers to the Blessed Virgin disallowed on Tuesday evening will be permitted on Thursday morning, when Stanford's 'Stabat Mater' is to be given. This, however, will be under the discreet veil of the Latin language.[20]

At this Festival Elgar conducted *The Kingdom* rather than *Gerontius*. It was suggested in the *Daily Telegraph* that this was due to his dissatisfaction at having to tamper with the text, 'and from a Catholic point of view he was, of course, right'.

Another conscientious objector was Gervase Elwes who, as a boy, had been a favourite pupil of Newman at the Oratory School. In 1908 he sang the part of Gerontius. It was only at a late stage that 'the Dean and Chapter had directed that the name of the Mother of God should be excluded from the text'. When Elwes was given this information it was too late for him to withdraw from the performance. But in 1920, receiving the instruction early, he announced that he would sing the work as it was written or not at all. He did not sing.

Gervase felt very strongly indeed about the whole business. He regarded the action of the Dean and Chapter as 'bigoted, inartistic and idiotic'.[21]

Notes

1 Rosa Burley papers; Basil Maine confirmed Elgar's reluctance; see *Edward Elgar: His Life and Works*, 2 vols, 1933, I, p 118.
2 . . . Nuper modorum musicorum arte quali Gerontii animam temporis in puncto minutissimo coeli per spatium infinitum leniter labantem descripsit, arte quali choros caelestes, 'laudem Deo in excelsis, laudem Deo in profundis' cantatantes induxit. Quotiem orchestrae totius e concentus quam admirabilem sonorum varietatem elecuit . . . .
3 AMZ 79 Niederrheinisssches Musikfest zu Düsseldorf.
4 Festival Committee members: Dean R W Frost; Canons B Cattley, W J Knox-Little, Melville, H H Woodward (Precentor); Bp Charles Gore (Chairman).

5   HWRO 705–445: 3347; responsibility in respect of copyright was with Father Neville.

6   HWRO 705–445: 3539.

7   HWRO 705–445: 3681.

8   Elgar's preference for the Sheffield chorus for the Coronation music displeased Frederick Spark, whose comments drew a sharp answer from J H Green, Hon Sec Leeds Philharmonic Soc.:

> '... What is the reason for this choice? Both choruses are Yorkshire voices and Leeds has the great advantage of an established reputation and experience. It must be either that Mr Elgar desires Dr Coward for his chorus master, with a younger, rawer chorus than Leeds, or that he, upon his own judgement deems the Sheffield chorus a better chorus than the Leeds chorus .... This is not partisanship but a sadly sober fact for Leeds chorus singers – it is Mr Elgar's judgement, and Mr Spark [Hon Sec Leeds Music Festival] does not like it and Leeds singers do not like it.' (copy in Leeds Public Library).

9   *BWJ*, 6 September.

10 Letter at Oratory.

11 Diary 11 and 12 September 1902.

12 HWRO 705–445: 3653.

13 HWRO 705–445: 3683: Denis Sheil, son of Sir Justin Sheil (1803–1871) Ambassador to Persia, friend of Cardinal Merry del Val and Pope Pius x. Denis was a pupil at the Oratory School.

14 HWRO 705–445: 3677; see *Mus T* 1943, vol 75, p 638 for note of presentation to Eaton, after ten years conductorship of the Birmingham Catholic Choral Society which has 'done much for the understanding and appreciation of the finest polyphonic music'.

15 HWRO 705–445: 3658.

16 Daniel Lysons etc. *Annals of 3 Choirs*, 1895, p 129.

17 Excerpt from *The Tablet.*' in the scrapbook, Elgar Birthplace.

18 *Catholic Monthly Register*, p 275.

19 *A Doorkeeper of Music*, p 140.

20 *Yorkshire Post*, 9 September 1908.

21 Elwes, Winifred and Gervase, *Gervase Elwes: a Biography*, London 1935, p 210–11 [My copy of the Worcester programme of 1932 still shows the excisions–PMY.]

11 'I Do Not Praise Choruses Indiscriminately'

As early as 1865 the idea of a metropolitan cathedral to be built in London as a monument to the lately deceased Cardinal Wiseman had been promoted at a public meeting presided over by Henry Edward Manning, Wiseman's successor. A considerable sum of money was quickly subscribed and land was bought, near the site of the present cathedral in Westminster. But Manning, while approving the project in principle, considered his first duty to be the provision of much needed new schools and orphanages in the archdiocese, so that it was left to Manning's successor, Herbert Alfred Vaughan, to give substance to the idea of a cathedral.

Vaughan, of an aristocratic and Catholic family already long established at Courtfield in Herefordshire, was educated at Stonyhurst and Downside, as well as in Rome, and became Bishop of Salford in 1872. After twenty years of devoted service there he was chosen as Manning's successor at Westminster and in 1893 was created cardinal. In the following year an architect, John Francis Bentley, was appointed to design a new catherdral for Westminster which, in Vaughan's words, was to be 'the head and the heart of the Church in England'.

As in the case of the Brompton Oratory, the chosen architect, John Francis Bentley, was a Catholic convert. A Yorkshireman with markedly independent views, Bentley enjoyed a reputation for fine work in the Victorian Gothic tradition, for the Church of England as well as the Catholic Church. The site at Westminster required that a new building should not compete with Gothic neighbours. Vaughan was inclined to a church in Italian basilican style. Bentley, however, having experimented with Byzantine ideas, now sought inspiration from that tradition for his new commission. Combining ideas from a familiar Italian Renaissance style with a Byzantian idiom, he developed a structure of striking originality, to prove ideal as an auditorium for large-scale musical performance as well as for the whole repertory of Catholic liturgical music. Bentley, who died in March 1902, did not live to see the end of his work. By this time, however, Vaughan had been so successful in raising funds that the main structure of the building was already complete.[1]

Soon after Bentley's appointment as architect, Vaughan had begun to plan a campaign to raise money for the completion of the project. So successful was he that the main structure of the cathedral was completed within eight years. It was Vaughan's intention that the cathedral should become a centre for the cultivation of sacred music. At first, in order to establish the daily singing of Divine Office, he considered the possibility of entrusting the duty to a choir of English Benedictines, but when this appeared impracticable, Vaughan briefly entertained the idea of bringing French Benedictines from Solesmes to Westminster. Finally, he accepted the impracticability of these schemes, and, in 1901, appointed Richard Runciman Terry, organist at Downside since 1896, to be organist and musical director at Westminster.

By this time – although the interior of the cathedral was unready for occupation – the magnificence of the structure could be appreciated. On Ascension Day 1902 the whole of the Divine Office and High Mass were sung in the adjoining Chapter Hall. Already Vaughan, who knew that he had not long to live, wrote on 15 May to his friend of long standing, the widowed Lady Herbert of Lea:

> We have twenty-five first-rate trebles and sixteen men, in addition to the clergy. I have formed a College of Cathedral Chaplains, not to exceed twenty-four, four of whom are called Prebendaries, and I have secured a Prebend for all. So that is a permanent arrangement that will last after I have gone.

The administration of the musical establishment of the cathedral was the responsibility of Monsignor Thomas Dunn.
Vaughan continued,

> Mgr. Dunn and Mr. Terry are deeply engaged in the musical performance to be given in the cathedral on June 11 – it is to be a very high class affair and they hope to make money enough to set up the Choir with music and other things for a long time to come. I am not sanguine that it will be a success.[2]

On 11 June Terry and Dunn, together with Edward D'Evry and Arthur Barclay, respectively organist and music director of Brompton Oratory, arranged a choral and orchestral concert to take place in the cathedral. 'The primary object of the performance', stated the programme, 'is to try the acoustic properties of the cathedral by a rendering of music of every period.' The programme included Wagner's *Das Liebesmahl der Apostel*, an ambitious cantata by Thomas Wingham, former music director at Brompton Oratory, and works by Palestrina, Byrd, Blow, Purcell and Bach.

The programme – which lasted for three hours – ended with Beethoven's Third Symphony.

The cardinal again accounted to Lady Herbert:

> The Cathedral Concert went off very well. It was too long and too metaphysically German – because too much of Wagner and Beethoven. But the motets were admirable: and all were assured that the church is good for sound both for the singer and the speaker. We ought to have made a lot of money for the Choir, but I fancy the expenses have run away with the profits.[3]

On 12 and 13 March 1903 the Elgars were in the Potteries, where a performance of *Gerontius* was to be given in Hanley Town Hall. Here Elgar had formerly played the violin in the North Staffordshire Festival orchestra and had conducted the first performance of *King Olaf*. Now, to mark his present eminence and the association of the choir with *Gerontius*, he was presented with a loving cup, locally potted, showing a laurel-wreathed composer and a prayerful Cardinal.

The principals on 13 March were Muriel Foster, John Coates, and David Ffrangcon-Davies, 'with Band and Chorus of 300 performers'. The band was strengthened by the inclusion of some forty players from the Hallé Orchestra. In the note of congratulation that he wrote to the Society afterwards Elgar said:

> The tone is magnificent – silvery yet solid, well-balanced & sonorous, and the 'attack', fine: the infinitesimal trifles – not shortcomings – which did occur were caused merely by the want of more time in rehearsing with the orchestra. I place the chorus in the highest rank & I thank the members for giving me the opportunity of hearing a performance of my work almost flawless.
>
> I do not praise choruses indiscriminately & I do not make comparisons because some choral societies and festivals are not so well served as Hanley in the matter of a concert room . . . .[4]

In those days when it was choral performances in the north that drew the critics from London, *The Athenaeum*, observing that 'the performance was much approved', drew attention to 'the pure and refined singing of the choir', and the fact that its members were 'drawn from the working folk of the Potteries'.

It was remarkable, and probably reprehensible, that as yet no London society had attempted a performance of *Gerontius*. Now it seemed that this situation might be repaired. On 15 March Alice wrote in her diary, 'E. had letters from Lady M. Warrender & Mrs S. Wortley both with schemes. One for gr[eat] Union Jack Concert, the other for *Gerontius* in the Westminster Cathedral'. With Mrs Wortley's letter came another, from Lady Mary Talbot, a lady conspicuous for her energetic promotion of social and educational schemes for the benefit of Catholics in London and in Sheffield. Her husband, Lord Edmund Talbot, brother of the fifteenth Duke of Norfolk, like the Duke, had been a pupil at the Oratory School, and also had known Newman.

The letters to which Alice referred concerned two possibilities of *Gerontius* being heard in the capital: the one during a projected Festival of English music, the other – with strong support from Lady Talbot – in Westminster Cathedral. In the latter case it would be an occasion for helping the funds of the cathedral. After a fine recent performance of *Gerontius* in Manchester, Schultz-Curtius, the London agent 'arranged with the Halle Executive and Richter to give the first London performance. For this concert the Hallé orchestra would be accompanied by the Manchester Choir of 250 voices'. It seems, however, that at this point Schultz-Curtius was taking too much for granted.

As he had strong family connections with Sheffield, the Duke of Norfolk drew attention to the reputation of the Choral Society of that city, of which the conductor was Henry Coward. Of this Elgar was well aware, for he had been especially moved by a brilliant performance of *Gerontius* which he had heard in Sheffield the previous October. However, in the end, his own preference in the matter of chorus was for the one he had recently worked with in the Potteries:

> The North Staffs Choral Society knows the work well – it is a very fine Chorus & sang Gerontius under my direction on Friday last. I fear a London chorus cd. not be got together without great trouble & it wd. require a tremendous amount of training. . . . If Lady Edmund Talbot can see any way to get a satisfactory chorus – and North Staffs is not more distant than Sheffield – the rest wd. be easy. Mr [John] Coates however must be the Gerontius.[5]

During March 1903 *Gerontius* was performed in Wolverhampton, Liverpool and Chicago (from where a 'delightful cablegram' reported success). At Liverpool, as at Manchester, the principal soloist was Ludwig Wüllner.

In the meantime the organization of a cathedral performance was entrusted to Hugo Görlitz and it was decided that the proceeds of the performance would be for the benefit of the Cathedral Choir School. As well as Schultz-Curtius, Elgar had been in favour of an invitation to take part in the performance being sent to the Hallé Orchestra. However, he was informed that the members of the orchestra were dispersed all over the place at various seaside resorts and London and would not assemble again until the Birmingham Festival.

At this point Görlitz approached the Concertgebouw Orchestra in Amsterdam, which was already engaged to come to London in June, for a Strauss Festival in which the young Willem Mengelberg was to share the conducting with Strauss. He also met Terry for the first time, and made arrangements to meet the administrator of the cathedral. Lady Talbot, who was keeping in close contact with all the parties involved, wrote to Elgar on 23 March:

> The Cardinal is still very ill I fear but I have sent him word as to what has been arranged so far. He is very anxious to have the performance properly carried out but is quite unable to discuss any business at present.[6]

The Talbots were very close to the cardinal and for some time in the previous year he had been a guest at their country home. He was, indeed, now very near to the end of his life. On 19 March he received the last sacraments, and on 25 March he left the archbishop's House at Westminster for St Joseph's College at Mill Hill.

A week later Görlitz met a representative of the cathedral chapter and learned that there was general agreement on everything concerning the performance. But on the musical side there were still problems to be solved. Görlitz told Elgar that he would willingly accept his suggestion as to the other soloists, but in respect of a contralto, he was obliged by contract to give the first refusal to a singer (unnamed) with whom he had a permanent agreement. If, however, she did not satisfy Elgar, Görlitz was quite willing to approach Muriel Foster. He was certain, however, that she would not give her services and he was resolute in refusing to 'employ anybody who does not give their services for such an occasion'.

Wüllner, who – in spite of his imperfect command of English – had won glowing reports from his performances at Manchester and Liverpool, had promised his services. Görlitz would at once write to invite David Ffrangcon-Davies. But Terry, it seems, was not pleased at being taken for granted. Görlitz confided to Elgar:

> There has been some difficulty with Mr Terry who has charge of the music in the cathedral as you know, because he wants his Choir to be employed too. In order to get out of the difficulty I suggested that they should do one of his works, & that his Choir should join the Staffordshire singers. He also said that you had promised to conduct the performance & if it is your desire to do so, I shall be only too pleased to arrange with Herr Mengelberg that he should cede the baton to you.[7]

Elgar remained firm that Muriel Foster should be engaged and advised that the cathedral singers should not be mixed with the North Staffordshire choristers. Görlitz managed to persuade Terry to abandon the idea of combining the choirs but had to agree that the cathedral choir should begin the performance with two pieces before *Gerontius*. In spite of Lady Talbot's diplomatic help no more concessions could be won from Terry, who was anxious to use the occasion to perform his edition of Tallis's *Lamentations*. After the Staffordshire choir had promised to come to

London on 6 June, Görlitz met a deputation to determine all the arrangements. It was settled that Elgar should conduct, but the choir asked to sing the Bach motet 'I wrestle and Pray' before *Gerontius*. At this point Terry insisted that it should be a condition that both choirs should sing Tallis's *Lamentations*.

On 6 April Görlitz was finding all this rather tiresome:

> Everything is not quite such smooth sailing as I thought. I was informed on Saturday that if I write a letter to the Vicar General undertaking the responsibility of the expenses, the arrangement could be proceeded with forthwith, but it seems that the *Vicar General* as Administrator of the Cathedral is a little hurt in his pride, because he was evidently not consulted at first, and the permission of the Cardinal was obtained before his.[8]

The Vicar General was duly mollified, the choirs were instructed that no music other than *Gerontius* would be performed, and both Ffrangcon-Davies and Muriel Foster – the latter writing from St Petersburg – pledged their presence for 6 June. Meanwhile, Lady Talbot continued to be very active throughout the proceedings and was anxious that the King should be approached as to the possibility of his attending the performance. She wrote to Elgar on 17 April:

> I have written to the Duke of Norfolk about the King. It is a matter which will requires delicate handling for many reasons, because there are difficulties about the King coming into a Catholic church in this country . . . .[9]

Edward VII, personally, was well disposed to Catholics, and – after a recent state visit to the King of Italy – he had taken the opportunity of paying 'a private and informal visit to the Vatican' to meet the 93-year-old Pope, Leo XIII. The preliminaries to this occasion had exhausted much high level discussion concerning the possible political disfavour that might ensue were the visit to take place. In respect of inviting the King to *The Dream of Gerontius*, the Duke of Norfolk decided that the best person to approach the King was Elgar himself. Whether he did so is not recorded.

On 21 April Görlitz had reported the bad news that the Amsterdam orchestra, without giving any reason, had now withdrawn from their engagement. Thus it was necessary to recruit players in London: the strings of the Philharmonic, and the woodwind of the Queen's Hall orchestra. Elgar's wealthy German friend, Henry Ettling – 'Uncle Klingsor' – had promised to play the timpani. The Strauss Festival was to take place between June 3 and 6, thus any other engagement in London was impossible.[10]

Four thousand circulars advertising the performance were distributed in April and, on Elgar complaining, Görlitz responded edgily, 'You do not seem to understand that when I undertake the risk of guaranteeing the expenses up to £1000 I must, to a certain extent, have a free hand in advertising'. He continued:

> ... With regard to the orchestra players, I do hope that you will not ask to send out of town for any artists. The expenses are already so enormous, especially now that the Amsterdam Orchestra will not take part. And I cannot contract any further liabilities in the matter. Mr. Frye Parker will be the First Violin, Mr. Eyres Principal Second, Mr. Ferrer Principal Viola, and Mr. Ould Principal 'Cello. With regard to the three last named Principals, I am quite willing to meet you if I can obtain the artists in question at the same fee as I have to pay here, namely £2.12.6. With regard to Mr. Squire, I would not engage him on any condition whatsoever. I strongly object to Mr. Squire being in any Orchestra that I engage.[11]

There were still difficulties to overcome. There was a tendency for soloists to avoid attending too many rehearsals. This was not very helpful to Görlitz, who wrote again to Elgar:

> I am obliged for your favour of yesterday's date & will do as you say about the rehearsals, but Dr Wüllner will not attend the rehearsal on Saturday morning, & it will be just as well if I have a substitute for Miss Foster on the Friday. In fact I think you owe me that, for I want to convince you that there are other artists who can sing the music quite as well as Miss Foster. Dr. Wüllner will rehearse his part on Friday afternoon, or will do without rehearsals altogether.[12]

On Saturday morning, 6 June, the journey of the choir to London began at 3.30 am. The special train provided by the North Staffordshire Railway Company left from Alsager, in Cheshire. Then, having stopped at every station through the Potteries, it joined the main line at Stoke. Choristers had difficulties in reaching the various stations at that time of the morning. Not perhaps surprisingly, the train was an hour late on arrival at Euston station, where James Whewall (who had travelled on the previous day) anxiously greeted his choristers and led them to a waiting omnibus. 'The drive through the fresh air through the streets sharpened the appetites of the singers', who, after breakfast at St James's Restaurant in Piccadilly, went to the cathedral for rehearsal.

The report of the afternoon performance in *The Musical Times* drew attention to Elgar's request for no applause:

> The setting of Cardinal Newman's poem by one who in religion and temperament is in perfect sympathy with it should naturally come under the special protection of the Roman Catholic community, and it was fitting if only from the point of view of sentiment, that it should be given in the great building which, when completed, is to be the cathedral church of their Archbishop.
> ... The crowd not only filled the nave, chapels, and side-aisles, but quite a large audience had seating accommodation in the apse behind the orchestra. As soon as Dr. Elgar was seen advancing to the front to take his place on the

rostrum the occupants of seats in the apse at the rear of the chorus commenced to clap. This Dr. Elgar immediately repressed, and thus this proved to be the only demonstration throughout the proceedings.[13]

The Tablet ended its notice of the occasion in this manner:

> And some day it may be the privilege of lovers of the highest and most concentrated art to hear High Mass sung in Westminster Cathedral [Wiseman would have said Westminster Abbey!], the music written by Dr. Elgar. We do not know of any great Mass written by a musician of the Wagnerian school. Dr. Elgar is a Catholic, and of musicians of today he is first. We think he owes it to the Church, to Art, and to himself, to write some day a great Mass which may serve to mark, to succeeding ages, the dawn of the twentieth century and the birth of the great fane of Westminster.[14]

Cardinal Vaughan died on June 19. The Requiem sung six days later was the first service to take place in the cathedral.

The remainder of June 1903 found Elgar occupied in completing *The Apostles*. Across the country people had taken *The Dream of Gerontius* to their hearts. The Three Choirs Festival was taking place in Hereford that year. On 3 September Elgar, accompanied by his friends Rodewald and Schuster,

> walked through the fields, bright sunny morning to Belmont. Heard Ite Missa Est to the tune of the Angel in *Gerontius*. Both men were much impressed by all they saw and heard. This beautiful church out in the country.

Ten days later with his wife and daughter Elgar went again to Belmont, to the church of the Benedictine monastery.

> The Litany was being chanted as we arrived, the same as in 'Gerontius'. Then we went in, lovely sunny day. After Mass, the Preacher came across to E. and asked to take him over the Monastery. We waited and the monks filed out. The grounds looked lovely. E. asked if he might go and stay there a week sometime. A glad consent.[15]

Since then *The Dream of Gerontius* has become a classic, in a sense that the subsequent oratorios, *The Apostles* and *The Kingdom*, have not. Given the fact that the work was a *succès d'estime* in Germany after its first performance in Düsseldorf and the bestowal of a general seal of approval by Strauss, and was popular with (mostly northern) choral societies for some years, it is remarkable that *Gerontius* carries special authority into modern times.

It was, of course, not only the creation of Elgar. Newman's poem in its own right, at its first publication, compelled a wide audience. It was Elgar's genius to perceive that within it was a dramatic scheme, the nature of which he instinctively understood and was able to translate.

Many of the greatest works of music have been inspired by the religions of the west. Elgar was educated in religion through the principles and practices of restored Catholicism, of which tradition *The Dream of Gerontius* is, in one sense, a celebration. This was symbolized on the one hand by Elgar's presentation of the original manuscript to the Oratory founded by Newman, on the other hand by the performance of the work in 1903 in the new cathedral in Westminster.

But the story of 'Gerontius' is older than Newman or Elgar.

The depth of the emotional response aroused by the work at one particular time is within a letter which Elgar would never see.

THE WHITE GATES,
WESTCOTT ROAD,
DORKING.

Feb [1934]

Dear Elgar

I want to tell you how my choirs of the Dorking Festival are loving performing 'Gerontius' – greatly daring I suggested it for this years [*sic*] festival – I had been longing to do it for years, but had thought it too dangerous an experiment as I could not bear to do it badly[.]

Whether we shall do it well I do not know [.] But if enthusiasm and hard work can achieve anything be sure that it will not lack these. And it will be one of the great moments of my life when I stand with trembling baton to conduct it. We have good soloists – Astra Desmond, Steuart Wilson and Harold Williams – and we shall think of you – please give us your blessing.

Of course this wants no answer

Yrs affectionately

R Vaughan Williams[16]

Notes

1 Funds from the sale of the site of the old cathedral of St Mary's, Moorfields, which lost its congregation through encroachment of commercial development, helped the new project.
2 *Letters to Lady Herbert of Lea*, 1902, n d, p 445. Thomas Dunn, b 1870, educated at Beaumont School and St Thomas's Seminary, Hammersmith, ordained by Vaughan in 1893, archbishop's staff from 1894 to 1903.
3 Ibid, p 446.
4 HWRO 705–445: 2992.

5   HWRO 705–445: 3845.

6   HWRO 705–445: 3769.

7   HWRO 705–445: 3851.

8   HWRO 705–445: 3854; presumably the vicar general was assuming the place of the cardinal at this time; he would not in the course of his normal duties be involved with events in the cathedral.

9   HWRO 705–445: 3774.

10 HWRO 705–445: 3875.

11 HWRO 705–445: 3859; Squire, William Henry (1871–1963), leading cellist in Queen's Hall, Covent Garden, and other orchestras. Recorded Elgar's Violoncello Concerto in 1930. The reason for Görlitz's dislike is not recorded.

12 HWRO 705–445: 3864.

13 *Mus T* vol 44, 1903, p 477.

14 *The Tablet*, 13 June 1903.

15 Diary 13 September; Belmont Abbey f 1850, the church being intended as the cathedral of the new diocese of Newport and Menevia, see 'The Founding of Belmont', *Downside Review*, v, 1886, p 232.

16 Broadheath MS 9413 (1); performance noticed in *Mus T*, 1934, vol 75, June issue, 'Music in the Provinces', p 553.

Appendix

Elgar Birthplace MSS 6–15

Consists of 161 sheets of the original material for *Gerontius* (short score) sent to Novello for engraving vocal scores and subsequently returned. In these Mss sheets are numerous variants of the initial material which itself had originated in pencil sketches which were not kept. Occasional bars were deleted, in others alterations were made in red ink. The state of such passages before alteration is given below, the effect of the alterations being best appreciated by reference to the published vocal score of the work. Although most of the markings represent only minor adjustments the effect sometimes is considerable. Nowhere is this more marked than in the conclusion of 'Praise to the Holiest in the Height' or after **120** where alterations were made after Jaeger's criticism of the original.

The material for Part I comprises: Prelude, and then sections between rehearsal numbers as follows 21–35, 35–57, 57–68, 68–end; for Part II, between 11–16, 75–89, 89–101, 101–126, 126–end.

Music examples Part I

2 bars before [rehearsal number] **4** [Ex. 1], 5 bars after **11** [Ex. 2],

[Ex. 1]   [Ex. 2]

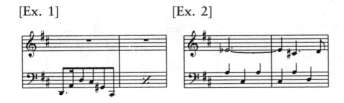

2 after **12** [Ex. 3]. 12 after **13** [Ex. 4], 3 after **18** [Ex. 5], at **22** [Ex. 6],

[Ex. 3]   [Ex. 4]   [Ex. 5]   [Ex. 6]

2 after **25** [Ex. 7], 5 after **26** [Ex. 8], 5 after **33** [Ex. 9],

[Ex. 7]   [Ex. 8]

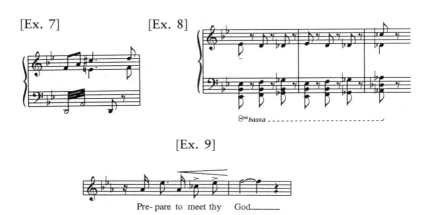

[Ex. 9]

5 after **36** [Ex. 10], 4 after **37** [Ex. 11], 4 after **48** [Ex. 12],

1 before **50** [Ex. 13], 6 after **50** [Ex. 14], 6 after **54** [Ex. 15],

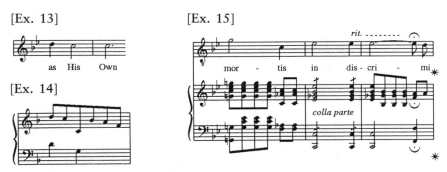

at **63** [Ex. 16], 4 after **63** [Ex. 17], 2 before **72** [Ex. 18],

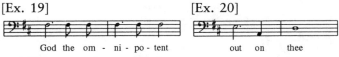

at **75** [Ex. 19], 1 before **76** [Ex. 20]:

[Ex. 19]

God the om - ni - po - tent

[Ex. 20]

out on thee

at **14** *con grandezza* added

4 bars after **16**, redistribution of keyboard parts on stave

8 bars after **54**, '* if desired the following recit may be omitted by going immediately to **63**'.

64: Semi-Chorus: 'Enoch and Elias from the common doom . . . Amen'

(next page) 'Noe from the waters in a saving home . . . Amen
Abraham from th'abounding guilt of Heathenesse; . . . Amen
David from Goliath and the wrath of Saul; . . . Amen'

Music Examples Part II

*4 after **100** [Ex. 1], 3 after **116** [Ex. 2],

[Ex. 1]

[Ex. 2]

8 after **120** [Ex. 3], 5 after **127** [Ex. 4], at **128** [Ex. 5],

[Ex. 3]

[Ex. 4]   [Ex. 5]

3 before *****131** [Ex. 6], **120**: Psalm 90 ('Lord Thou hast been our refuge') precedes Gerontius, 'Take me away'

[Ex. 6]

Occasionally particular marks of expression and other miscellaneous information were idiosyncratically indicated:

Part I
3 before **6** <afflictando> apassionato
9 after **40** angosciosamente <disperato>
2 after **66** <lento> Andante/ plintivo e mistico
         68 solenne e con esultazione
         70 poco più lento / egualmente

On a blank side page 40, preceding cue 72:

* '*Name* must have a capital where it refers to any One of the Trinity / It is printed so in most edns the one I sent is wrong in this case'.

p 45: '*Note.* in *most* edns of the poem the word of *Name* has a cap – I think it is l.c. in the particular edn I sent for the printer – but that one is wrong. E.E.'

Part II

11–16, inscription after **16**, 'For Mrs. Jaeger' [to whom a daughter was born on 26 April 1900]. Mrs Jaeger, formerly Isabella Donkerley, was a violin student at the Royal College of Music in 1898.

Full Score of *The Dream of Gerontius*

This is in the possession of the Oratory of St Philip Neri, Edgbaston, Birmingham. The title page is inscribed, 'Birchwood, In Summer, 1900' and is signed by Charles Beale, Lord Mayor of Birmingham; G H Johnstone, Chairman of the Birmingham Musical Festival; Marie Brema, Edward Lloyd and Plunkett Greene; the last pages of the score 302–304 have a symbolic representation of Elgar, Alice and Carice Elgar, the signatures of the orchestral players, as well as of Anthony Newman, Orchestral Attendant, A J Jaeger ('ye humble Analyst'), and W Dodd ('ye lowly copyist').

Part I

Prelude: extra Percussion, marked 'Batteria', 3 after **2** – 'Prayer' above stave; 3 before **6**, 'miserere' below stave; after **7** 'Celli / Despair'; **9** 'Despairissimo', **12** 'Go forth in the name of the Apostles and Evangelists' below stave; 1 before **17** 'Death' at **17** 'Sleep /[crotchet] = 66, 5 after **17** 'Fear' below stave; **19** 'Miserere' below stave; **20** 'Judgment' below stave; **36** Vl 2, 'original for vla.' for 2 bars; at *Allegro* before **55**, '<Presto>' above stave; at **64** 'Swell 8ft only' above stave; 3 after **73** <'vl 1,2 formerly Va'>.

Part II

3 before **16**, 'at Birchwood Lodge in Summertime' below stave; at **42**, ('Birchwood Lodge in Thunderstorm'). Between **61** and **71** proof sheets of vocal score are pasted in.

Bibliography

Atterbury, Paul, Wainwright, Clive (1994) (eds), *Pugin – A Gothic Passion*, Exhibition Catalogue, Victoria and Albert Museum, New Haven/London: Yale UP.

Bailey, Cyril (1935), *Religion in Virgil*, Oxford: Oxford University Press.

Bence-Jones, Mark (1992), *The Catholic Families*, London: Constable.

Biener, Günter (1989), *John Henry Newman: Leben und Werk*, Mainz: Matthias-Grünewald-Verlag.

Brooks, Michael W. (1987), *John Ruskin and Victorian Architecture*, New Brunswick: Rutgers U Press/London: Thames & Hudson.

Butler, Charles (1822), *Historical Memoirs of the English, Irish, and Scottish Catholics since the Refomation*, 4 vols, London: John Murray.

Butler, Edward C. (1926), *The Life and Times of Bishop Ullathorne, 1806–1889*, 2 vols, London: Burns Oates & Co.

Cauchi, Simon (1991) (ed.), *The Sixth Book of Virgil's Aeneid, translated by Sir John Harington (1604)*, Oxford: Clarendon Press.

Clark, G. Kitson (1973), *Churchmen and the condition of England 1812–1885*, London: Methuen.

Cowden-Clarke, Mary Victoria (1896), *My Long Life*, London: T Fisher Unwin.

Edwards, David L. (1971), *Leaders of the Church of England 1828–1944*, OUP, London.

Faber, Frederick William (1857), *Poems*, 2nd ed, London: R Richardson & Co.

Farrell, John K A (1967), *The Church of St Anselm and St Cecilia*, Bristol: Burleigh Press.

Ferrey, Benjamin (1861), *Recollections of A N Welsby Pugin and his Father*, Appendix by E Sheridan Purcell, London.

Ffinch, Michael (1991), *Cardinal Newman – The Second Spring*, London: Weidenfeld and Nicolson.

Fuller, Reginald Cuthbert et al (1956), *Warwick Street Church: An Outline of the History of the Church of Our Lady of the Assumption and St Gregory, formerly the Royal Bavarian Chapel*, London.

Gillow, Joseph (1885), *A Literary and Biographical History, or, Bibliographical Dictionary of the English Catholics*, London: Burns & Oates.

Guiney, Louise Imogen (1904), *Hurrell Froude, Memoranda and Comments*, London: Methuen.

Gwynn, Denis (1946), *Lord Shrewsbury, Pugin and the Catholic Revival*, Catholic Book Club, London: Hollis & Carter.

Holt, G (1854), *The English Jesuits 1650–1829, A Biographical Dictionary*, Catholic Record Society.

Hurd, Michael (1981), *Vincent Novello – and Company*, London: Granada

Husenbeth, F C (1860), *The Life of the Right Reverend Monsignor Weedall DD*, London: Longmans & Co.

Hutchings, Arthur (1967), *Church Music in the Nineteenth Century*, London: Jenkins.

Hyatt King, A. (1963), *Some British Collectors of Music c 1600–1960*, Cambridge: The University Press.

Jones, Rev James (1845), *A Manual of Instructions /or/ Plain Chant, or Gregorian Music, wih the Chants as used in Rome*, London.

Kelly, Rev Bernard W (1903), *A Short History of St George's Cathedral and the Diocese of Southwark*, London.

Kerr, Ian (1990), *John Henry Newman, A Biography*, Oxford University Press.

Laing, Robert C (1895), *Ushaw College, A Centenary Memorial*, Newcastle-on-Tyne.

Little, W J Knox (1897), *St Francis of Assisi – His Times, Life and Work*, Lectures at Worcester Cathedral, Lent 1896, London.

Mack, Maynard (1985), *Alexander Pope: A Life*, New Haven: London.

Martin, Brian (1982), *John Henry Newman: His Life & Work*, London: Chatto & Windus.

Milner, Rev John (1811), *A Treatise on the Ecclesiastical Architecture of England, During the Middle Ages*, London: J Taylor, Architectural Library.

Minskip, Dominic (1989), *A History of St Wilfrid's Mission, York (1742 to the Present)*, [St Wilfrid's Church] York.

Mozley, J B (1882), *Reminiscences chiefly of Oriel College and the Oxford Movement*, London: Longmans.

Mozley, J B (1885), *Letters of the Rev J B Mozley, DD*, edited by his sister, London: Rivingtons.

Muirhead, J H (1909), (ed.), *Nine famous Birmingham Men*, Birmingham: Cornish.

Navarro, Mary Anderson de (1936), *A Few More Memories*, London.

Noake, John (1861), *A History of the Roman Catholics and Dissenters of Worcester*, Longmans & Co., London/Worcester.

Norman, Edward (1984), *The English Catholic Church in the Nineteenth Century*, Oxford: Oxford University Press.

Pattinson, Mark (1885), *Memoirs*, London: Macmillan.

Pugin, Augustus Northmore Welby (1837), *An Apology for a Work entitled 'Contrasts'*, Birmingham.

———— (1843), *An Apology for the Revival of Christian Architecture in England*, London.

———— (1843), *The Present State of Ecclesiastical Architecture in England*, republished from *The Dublin Review*, London.

———— (1850), *An Earnest Appeal for the revival of the ancient Plain Song*, London.

Purcell, E Sheridan (1900) (ed and finished by Edwin de Lisle) *Life and Letters of Ambrose Phillips de Lisle*, Macmillan, London.

Scott, Sir (George) Gilbert (1879), *Lectures on the Rise and Development of Mediaeval Architecture*, 2 vols, John Murray, London.

Snead-Cox, Herbert Daniel (1910), *The Life of Cardinal Vaughan*, 2 vols, London: Burns & Oates.

Sparrow, John (1967), *Mark Pattison [1813–1884] and the Idea of a University*, CUP. Cambridge.

Stasny, John and Nelson (1990–91), *Byron: 'From Dream to Dream: The Dream of Gerontius* by John Henry Newman and Edward Elgar, *Renascence*, XLIII, nos 1–2, Milwaukee 53233.

Sugg, Joyce (1983) (ed), *A Packet of Letters: A Selection from the Correspondence of John Henry Newman*, Oxford.

Thom, John Hamilton [1841], (ed), *The Life of the Rev Joseph Blanco White . . .*, 3 vols, London.

Trappes-Lomax, Michael (1932), *Pugin: A Mediaeval Victorian*, London: Sheed & Ward.

Trappes-Lomax, Michael (1936), *Bishop Challoner, A Biographical Study*, London: Longmans & Co.

Tristram, Henry (1933), *Newman and his Friends*, John Lane, London.

———— (1945), *Introduction: John Henry Newman, Centenary Essays*, London.

———— (1956), *John Henry Newman, Autobiographical Writings*, London/New York: A C Black.

Ullathorne, William B (1891–2), *The Autobiography of Archbishop Ullathorne, with Selections from his Letters*, Burns & Oates, London.

Upton, Arthur John (1981), *Oscott College and the Education of the*

Catholic Gentry in the Nineteenth Century, M Ed Diss, University of Birmingham.

Williams, Michael E (1979), *The Venerable English College, Rome,* London.

Annual Register, The

Birmingham Daily Post, 1903.

Birmingham Faces and Places ii, 1890.

Catholic Gentleman's Magazine, The, London, 1818.

Catholic Magazine and Review, The, ii, 1832.

Catholic Record Society xxxviii: Registers of the Catholic Chapels Royal/ and of the / Portuguese Embassy Chapel 1662–1829 (vol i Marris), London, 1941.

Gentleman's Magazine, The

Musical Times, The

Musical World, The

Orthodox Journal and Catholic Monthly Intelligencer, The, vol v London, 1817.

Oscottian, The, St Mary's College, Oscott; ii, no 1 (1901), vi, no 1 (1905), viii, no 3 (1908), ix, no 3 (1909), new series 1946, p 16.

Quarterly Musical Magazine, The

'St Chad's Cathedral, Birmingham, A History, 1841–1904', compiled by the Cathedral Clergy, 1904.

St George's Church, Worcester, Registers of Baptisms, Marriages and Deaths, (1) 1685–1778, (2) 1778–1797, (3) 1837–, (4) Burials, 1828–

Stockley's Concert Programmes 1870–95, 2 vols, Birmingham Public Library.

'Worcestershire Lives', by C A M Press [W Leicester, Printer, 6 High Street, Worcester].

Index